D0458100

THE
SWITCHING
HOUR

WHAT EXPERTS SAY ABOUT
THE SWITCHING HOUR

"Children deserve to have their parents read this book."
—**Gary Direnfeld**, MSW, RSE, Interaction Consultants
and I Promise Program, Inc., Ontario, Canada

"In this book, Dr. Flesberg makes the point that children in divorce have feelings. They are more than just chess pieces to be moved around to satisfy the needs or demands of the parents. The painful and poignant stories in this book, told from the perspective of a child, should help parents, attorneys, judges, mediators, and counselors understand how to consider children more in their plans. She makes it clear the traumatic toll on children is all too real. Dr. Flesberg gives many good suggestions and thought-provoking ideas to help parents and children post-divorce."
—**Marietta Shipley**, The Mediation Group of Tennessee, LLC, Nashville, Tennessee

THE
SWITCHING
HOUR

KIDS OF DIVORCE
SAY GOOD-BYE AGAIN

EVON O. FLESBERG

Abingdon Press
Nashville

THE SWITCHING HOUR
KIDS OF DIVORCE SAY GOOD-BYE AGAIN

Copyright © 2008 by Evon O. Flesberg

This book is printed on acid-free paper.

Library of Congress Cataloging-in-Publication Data

Flesberg, Evon O., 1954–
    The switching hour : kids of divorce say good-bye again / by Evon O. Flesberg.
      p. cm.
    ISBN 978-0-687-64976-1 (binding: printed/casebound : alk. paper)
    1. Children of divorced parents—Psychology. 2. Children of divorced parents—Attitudes. 3. Children of divorced parents—Family relationships. 4. Divorce—Psychological aspects. I. Title.

HQ777.5.F57 2007
306.874—dc22

2007029161

All scripture quotations unless noted otherwise are taken from the New Revised Standard Version of the Bible, copyright 1989, Division of Christian Education of the National Council of the Churches of Christ in the United States of America. Used by permission. All rights reserved.

The Switching Hour: Kids of Divorce Say Good-bye Again is a Switching Hour™ Series publication.

08 09 10 11 12 13 14 15 16 17—10 9 8 7 6 5 4 3 2 1

MANUFACTURED IN THE UNITED STATES OF AMERICA

CONTENTS

ACKNOWLEDGMENTS

Each NFL team has eleven named players on the field, but is supported by thousands. You who are the unnamed "twelfth player" have helped carry me beyond my own limits.

Thanks to you:

- My research assistant, Ken Jackson, attorney and mediator
- Janelle, Bob, and Lucy for quiet places
- Volney, Ken, Victor, Mary, Larry, April, Judd, Ryan, Cos, Matt, Beth, Norm, Sharon, Ev, and Bud for comments on drafts
- Abingdon Press—Kathy Armistead, John Kutsko, Barbara Dick, and Rick Schroeppel for catching the vision
- Norm for being the loving constant

> Peace to all children of the switching hour;
> you know who you are.

INTRODUCTION

"I liked yesterday,
  I don't like today,
  And there's nothing anyone can do
  about it."

He looked at me with dark brown eyes, wide and sorrow-filled, as he slowly and emphatically spoke these words. Life as he knew it for seven short years was over. There was no going back—no way to change what had happened. Mommy and Daddy got a divorce.

Nothing *he* could do about it. Nothing *I*, his counselor, could do about it. Nothing *his mother*, who sat on the couch beside him with tears sliding down her cheeks, could do about it. He liked yesterday. He doesn't like today. And there's nothing anyone can do about it. The years of the switching hour had begun.

Now Jimmy has two homes: two sets of parents, four adults who tell him what to do instead of two. He will have to say good-bye again and again.

With suitcase (or duffle bag, grocery sack, or black garbage bag) in their hands, you will see the children of the switching hour at the McDonald's and grocery store parking lots, and even maybe in the police station, on Friday evenings . . . and again on Sunday evenings. At least two times a month, and sometimes midweek too, children switch parents, homes, siblings, friends, pets, playthings, clothes, food, beds—and so much more.

If you look closely, you will see the children of the switching hour at airports when school is just out or is about to begin. Summer may be spent with Dad; when it's time for school, it's time for life with Mom, again. Around their shoulders will be the arms of the airline employees steering them through the maze of airport corridors and gate changes. Maybe you will sit beside the child who travels from Minnesota to New York so that she is able to have two parents in her life instead of one. You notice the children sometimes looking quite exhausted as they make extra trips at the holidays so everyone will get to celebrate—so no parent will be left out; no half brother or stepsister will be forgotten.

Statistics tell us that each year more than 1 million children join the switching hour life; at least 18–20 million children under the age of eighteen live divided lives. What do all those hours of going between households bring? *The Switching Hour: Kids of Divorce Say Good-bye Again* considers what the regular switching of homes means in the lives of young people. What is it like for them to live between parents in the switching hour?

Being between—leaving one place and moving toward, but not yet arriving in the new place—is called being in a *liminal* place. Look at a doorway; the piece of wood or metal across the bottom is called the *limen* in Latin. At that point, one is between spaces—neither in nor out. Psychologically, physically, and spiritually, the experience of liminality is a difficult one. Think about your time as a teenager. You were no longer a child but were not yet an adult. Children who experience the separation or divorce of their parents will spend years moving between them. It is not a single period of time dedicated to adjusting to the new experience of separated parents. The switching between parents continues for as many years as the parents are alive and the child continues to travel in order to be with each of them.

As you read this book, some of the stories may cause you to feel pain and sorrow. You may say, "That's not true for *my* child!" However, even the most upsetting stories are true for *many* children. More children than we would like to acknowledge wait to be part of the lives of *both* of their parents. The pain of waiting and wanting to know that a parent thinks about them at all shapes the lives of most children. It may not seem possible to you, a good and concerned parent, that many children visit parents who have addiction issues, anger problems, and mental illnesses that are severe but not sufficient to keep them from spending time with their children. These stories are intentionally included because those children have the most difficult time communicating what life is like for them in the hours they spend with that troubled parent. Having read and thought about *all* of these experiences may help you be a more caring adult for those children whom you may meet in your life.

I do not believe that being divorced or separated makes a person a bad parent. It will make life more complicated and, possibly, more stressful, both for you and your children. Research has shown that many changes cause stress and may contribute to illness. The changes may be positive as well as negative, unwanted and wanted. A story is told about good parents who divorced and who had the money to provide the same living conditions—same toys, clothes, music—in both homes. On one occasion, the child wanted a pair of shoes that were at Dad's house. Thinking that just buying an identical pair would take care of it, the mother offered to take the child to the store immediately. When the child said that it wouldn't help at all, the parents knew that it wasn't about the shoes! It wasn't about the shoes; it was about the feelings of the child. It's about the feelings of the children: feelings for which they don't always have words. They have feelings of guilt . . . thinking they might have caused your divorce. Feelings of sadness, grief, worry, and anger fill their hearts. They are upset about the loss of time with the other parent. Older children may feel as though they don't know who they are anymore. This is not how life was supposed to be. Their minds are occupied with what might happen next. This is all the more reason to turn our full attention to what the children in this book have to say.

For over twenty-five years as a pastor, pastoral counselor, adjunct professor in a divinity school, and in my life beyond work, I have heard stories about incredible suffering *and* strength, courage, and hope—from kids, parents, grandparents, and friends—about traveling between separated or divorced parents. We all have our own stories. Now for a moment stop and turn your heart just to the children. Let's stop and listen to children of the switching hour as they speak directly to us. Perhaps the children in your life might want to say something to you through them.

I have woven the threads from many different lives into these stories in order to share the truth of the stories that were told in my hearing. In the weaving, details have been changed or left out to protect those who spoke. The resulting stories may sound familiar to you; children often have common responses to the separation or divorce of parents and the life of traveling between them.

Experiences of loss, change, and constant transition are difficult for all of us. Talking about them lightens the load. *The Switching Hour: Kids of Divorce Say Good-bye Again* can help you and your family do just that. It is my hope that this book will help you have conversations with your children as well as the other parent. It will also suggest some things to do that may help bring more peace and less stress into your switching hour life.

Read this book in a way that is most helpful to you. You may want to read a chapter and then work through the suggestions in chapter 8 "How Can I Help?" before reading the next chapter; or you may wish to read the book straight through and then work with "How Can I Help?"

The book has eight chapters. The first chapter, *The Switching Hour,* is the foundation. The experiences of loss, change, and constant transition between parents are explored. The "switching hour" refers to the clock time when transitions take place. The phrase is also used as a metaphor, or shorthand way of speaking, about life lived with parents who are no longer together and what is required of their child because of it.

The second chapter, *The Hour I Wait and Long For*, addresses the missing and longing children have for the parent that they are not currently "visiting" and the inward excitement that mounts as the hour approaches to see that parent once again. They ask, "Can I be so lonesome and not hurt the parent I am with? How come I'm always sad?"

The third chapter, *The Hour I Hope Comes, But Does Not*, seeks to express the feelings and experiences of those children for whom the switching hour rarely or never comes. It describes the yearnings of children for painful realities to change: for example, about half of fathers have very little contact with their children after one year of a divorce (see Betty Carter and Monica McGoldrick, *The Expanded Family Life Cycle* [Needham Heights, Mass.: Allyn and Bacon, 1999], 14). The chapter focuses on what breaking promises does to a child's ability to trust and willingness to risk.

Chapter 4 is *The Hour I Wish Wouldn't Come.* It discusses required visitation of a parent with whom the child has conflict. We hear children's experiences of worry and dread in these situations. The chapter further explores leaving, traveling alone, the day of remarriage or a new partnership, another divorce, and more.

The Hour I Try To Avoid is chapter 5. It is a reflection on the choices children make as they grow up with the switching hour as their daily experience. They ask, "How can I endure the switching hour when I have fighting parents?" "How will I avoid the shuttling between parents when I am old enough to choose for myself?" The chapter looks at decisions they might make as older teenagers and young adults. It also addresses the difference it can make in how they conceive of marriage and family for themselves.

Chapter 6 is *The Hour I Spend with God*. Here we ponder the significance of the switching hour for children's spirituality. What are their images of God? How do they relate to their parents' faith lives?

The seventh chapter, *The Switching Hour Revisited*, suggests additional ways can all can make the switching hour lives of children and teenagers more bearable.

Chapter 8, *How Can I Help?* offers practical ideas and space for you to explore your own answers to that pressing question. Here you will find ways to help make life simpler, to ease the stress of many transitions and good-byes, and to be parents who can say WE CARE!

In each chapter you will hear about and from the children of the switching hour. There are also suggestions about how to help children negotiate what may be years of continual transitions and frequent good-byes. The one thing I want you to remember as you turn your heart and mind toward listening is that children have a great capacity for hope and love, and yes, even forgiveness. Reading this book shows them that you care about them. Even if they aren't able to talk with you about all of this right now, your children will know that you have taken time to look at life from their point of view and they will be encouraged by that. The children will feel supported when they tell you good-bye, knowing that they are loved and carried in your heart when you are apart.

CHAPTER ONE

THE SWITCHING HOUR

Dear Daddy,
I miss you!
I cry at night in my bed so Mama doesn't get sad.
Are you OK? Where do you sleep?
When will I see you? Mama said you'd meet me at McDonalds next Friday.
Don't forget!
Love,
Me

ONE BLUE DAY

Imagine that on a bright blue sunny day, you are told that from now on your family will have two homes instead of one. And the second house isn't a summer home. Your loved ones will always be in different places. You're an adult, so you say, "I've seen a lot of people go through a divorce or breakup." After whatever negotiating is necessary, you gather the things that have been declared yours and you start over. "Yes, it's painful. I miss my kids when they're not here, but I'm glad that I do not have to be in the midst of daily tension with my kids' other parent." Time helps the hurt.

Now enter a child's body; you are told that both of your parents will no longer be living in the place that you've been calling home. Two people whom you love intensely will now live in different places. When you come home from school, you know that only one parent's belongings will be there. The music, clothes, books, pets, and treasures of the other parent will have been removed. The child asks, "Do they think I won't be reminded by all the empty spaces that they left in our house? The silence is deafening after years of my parents talking, laughing, crying, and fighting. Our life has been split in two."

There's more. Now your parents want you to spend time with both of them, but in two different places. You will move between two parents' homes until you are no longer under their custody. Your healing will not come easily. You will constantly be reminded of the tension and hurt that caused this two-world existence in the first place. Like the

Bible story, you are the baby whom Solomon threatened to divide when two women each claimed it as her own. You have been divided. Where is your home? With Mom? With Dad? Between them at some midpoint? Like the writer of the "Dear Daddy" letter at the beginning of this chapter, you will miss your absent parent; you may try to hide your sadness, and you will beg not to be forgotten.

WHAT IS THE SWITCHING HOUR?

As a child, unlike your parents who ended their partnership and who no longer have to see each other except when they drop you off or on the occasional big event, you will travel like an astronaut between their two planets for many years. The years of the switching hour have begun. You will leave one parent's home, launch into the space between, and then enter the world of the other.

The switching hour is the *time and experience of leaving* one parent's home in order to be in the other parent's home at intervals decided by the parents or by the courts, most often without the input of children. The switching hour is also used as a *metaphor*, or shorthand way of speaking, about a *way of life* when parents are no longer together. Preparation for shuttling between parents—the many switching hour missions—will require no less attention than the space missions themselves. The pressures of launching and re-entry may feel as treacherous on the ground as they are in space travel.

TWENTY MILLION TRAVEL BETWEEN TWO WORLDS

Consider this, nearly half of first marriages end in divorce. Sixty percent of second marriages end in divorce. The result is that each year more than 1 million children in the United States become children of divorced or separated parents. That means at least 20 million children live the switching hour life. In addition, adult children of divorce and their children travel between parents, though normally not as frequently.

While their parents may be happier individually, the children still reside emotionally in the place between them. The divorce does not end, but rather begins, a life of additional stress for a child. What can be done to ease the pressure on children, who just by the fact they are children are already going through changes in their lives as they grow and mature?

Loving parents are troubled by stress in their children. What are you able to do? How can you help? In this book, I ask you to begin by paying closer attention to your child. Enter your child's mind. Try to imagine life as your child lives it. Listen to them and watch carefully. Though it may be difficult and uncomfortable for you, it is important to be aware of what happens to children as they enter the switching hour way of life.

LEARNING TO TRAVEL BETWEEN WORLDS

As you and your children learn what this new life will be like, the children may have mixed or confused feelings.

Children often feel guilty, thinking they caused the separation or divorce. Sometimes they may be relieved that the divorce they saw coming is finally over. They may be angry and blame one or both parents. They might feel nothing—just numbness. Whatever else they feel, as the reality of their divided lives sinks in, they will mourn their losses.

LOSS—a one-word description of all that follows from the announcement on that one blue day: "Sit down kids. Your dad and I have something to tell you. Everything's going to be okay, but your dad and I are breaking up. He's moving out tonight. Yes, we'll make sure you get to see him often. And of course, we'll split holidays."

WHAT ARE THE LOSSES?

I miss seeing both parents every day

For some children the sense of safety is lost and they are unable to rest; no longer knowing that both parents are safe and present, ready to defend and protect them from any danger. It means that there is half the amount of attention and energy to be shared with the child, even though the combined time available may have been brief when a child had two parents in the home.

A child had twice the possibility of being understood when she or he had two parents in the home. The temperament and personality of a child may more closely match that of his or her father rather than that of the mother. When it was time for setting rules and boundaries, a good cop–bad cop team created a sense that the children still had one parent "on their side."

I miss my home or having one place to call home

When parents separate, it is not uncommon for the family home to be sold. The parents don't want the memories, can't afford the mortgage, want to relocate to a new city, or to downsize; so there are often two new houses or apartments that the child will call home.

I miss my BIG family

For the kids who have had grandparents as a regular part of their lives, the grief and loss of missing them is more pain on top of pain. "Grandma babysat me until I was five. Then Mom and Dad divorced. Mom and I moved to the other coast. I didn't see my Grandma again until I was fifteen and she was dying. Mom let me fly back to see her. I cried and cried when she told me how much she had missed me all these years."

The grandparents, aunts, uncles, and cousins in one or both parents' families often disappear from the child's life after a split. For those of you in this place, you know it isn't always because travel is difficult or because there has been any alienation from your relatives. Often you say there's just so little time, you don't want to share the precious moments with anyone. Still, the children of the switching hour lose grandparents, aunts, uncles, and cousins.

I miss seeing my best friends all the time

Friends of all ages help us through life's rough spots. Think of your best friend for a minute. Did you smile?

When children experience their parents' breakup, friends are those to whom they turn for reassurance that everyone who cares about them has not left. Their friends tell them that they will be okay or what divorce is like for them.

Then another announcement comes. Although Mom has her new apartment, Dad and son are moving out of the city for the country life Dad has always wanted. It's time for Dad to make a new start, but the new beginning for Dad means more endings and losses for the child.

> "How will I ever make new friends when these kids have been together since they were five? We're in high school now; I'm not a jock, hardly a stud! Who'll sit with me at lunch? Life sucks!"
> —*OR*—
> "My old friends didn't seem excited to see me anymore when I went back for the holidays with Mom. I guess I wasn't that important to them after all. I miss my buddies and all the good times we had."

I miss my old school

Mom and Dad's split often means a move and a new school for the children. With all the other changes happening in their lives, there is pressure to make new friends, establish themselves in new clubs and on new ball teams, as well as to adjust to new teachers and new school buildings. It makes figuring out what they want to do when they grow up and where they want to attend college overwhelming for many. They worry about the future. College? Is there still money for that?

I've left the neighborhood

> "I loved running up the street for the ice cream truck, past the empty lot where we played ball,

past my best friend's house, by my first grade teacher's house and her flowerbeds. I could tell you the history of my first ten years running up that street. Then it was over. Dad found a new love. He didn't want to pay a big mortgage on two houses in nice subdivisions, soooo—good-bye, sweet memories. I live in an apartment on the other side of town."

Consider all that is familiar about where you are living. You know how quickly you can pick up the milk you need, where to rent the best DVDs, where you can get the juiciest hamburger, and where the fiercest dogs are in your walk around the block. These are parts of your daily surroundings that you take for granted. When the children of the switching hour move, all of that is lost. In half the time, or less, they often have to become familiar with *two* new neighborhoods, so that they can feel at home in each. The life the children expected is gone.

Now I don't know if there's enough money

The sense of financial security can be lost. For the children of the switching hour, there is often a profound shift in their household finances. If they're in the custody of their mothers, their standard of living will for the most part be lower than before the breakup. Some report that after a divorce the finances available to women are "reduced by 15 to 30 percent" whereas income of fathers "often remains the same or increases or decreases slightly" (Carter and McGoldrick, *The Expanded Family Life Cycle*, 391).

"Before my parents' divorce, I never worried about money. Suddenly, I wasn't sure if there would be money for my sports equipment or not. I'd ask Mom, and she'd say she was paying Dad enough child support for that, too. Then she'd want to know just how he was spending all the money she was sending. I couldn't tell her. Sometimes I feel guilty, like all these money problems are because of me and my kid brother and our child support payments. I hear about this at both houses."

I've lost the feeling that everything's going to be okay

The separation of parents changes a child's whole world. Mom and Dad could fix what went wrong; now Mom and Dad *are* what has gone wrong. The child wonders, "What else will happen to me? Why aren't we going to Disneyland this year? We planned that last summer. Now when I'm away from my other parent, I worry about him or her. What will happen next? Will they want me to come back? Will they meet someone new with kids? Will I have to share my room? That's what happened to my friend, Pete. I don't want to hurt like this ever again. Maybe it's better not to trust again. I don't want love to hurt this much."

Loss is difficult even if the future looks bright. Kids expect things to change, but often are not prepared for the long-term consequences when their parents break up, such as the pain of missing the absent parent, having separate holidays, or worrying about money for living expenses. As a parent you can help your children by anticipating what may lie ahead.

THE SADNESS AND GRIEF MAY END, BUT IT MIGHT TAKE A LONG TIME

There is *nothing* a child can do about the breakup of his or her parents' relationship. Unlike the couple that separates once, the child has repeated experiences of reuniting and separating. The leaving and grieving continue. For the children, each visit may reawaken the missing, the longing, and the hurt.

They do not want to be away from a parent. They are always "visiting," bonding ever tighter, then leaving again and loosening the bond. The phone calls, e-mails, letters, and pictures do not fill the parental hole that only a warm embrace and face-to-face conversation can fill.

"I'm always missing somebody." These are the words of a sixteen-year-old boy who traveled between parents (Nick Sheff, "My Long-Distance Life," *Newsweek*, February 19, 1999). This phrase captures the essence of the life lived between two parents. Where's the peace and comfort of being at rest?

SUPERMAN WOULD UNDERSTAND—I BELONG IN TWO WORLDS, TOO

If you have been unwillingly transferred to another country for your work, you understand the sudden shift that happens in a child's life. Deployed military personnel know life in two worlds well. There's the one you're in and the one you're missing.

The children of the switching hour also dwell in two worlds—Mom's World and Dad's World. The children no longer have roots that are allowed to go deep into one place, nurtured and tended by Mom and Dad. The roots are pulled out, "packed in burlap," and the tender tree is shipped back and forth. They now live as those who have left a "home country" for a new land (Jeanne Stevenson-Moessner, "Cross-cultured Children: Honoring Multiculturality." Lecture, Society for Pastoral Theology, Los Angeles, June 21, 2003).

"In Dad's world, life is full of travel with the band. We see such cool places and the people treat me like I'm a prince. I eat whatever I want and go to bed when everyone else crashes at night. When I want something, I tell them to put it on Dad's tab. I don't see Dad up close too much, but I go to all the concerts. He's usually tired or rehearsing some part of the gig when he has free time. Still, I want to be a musician when I'm an adult. He said I play the drums pretty well. In Mom's world, school is first. Mom is mad I didn't go to summer school to make up the English I flunked. Dad's done well without high school—I think I will too. Can't help she's the brainy-type who loves school. Her world is school, Dad's is music. I'm missing Mom. Funny, when I'm with her, I think nothing would make me happier than life on the road with Dad."

I DIDN'T SIGN UP TO BE VOICE MAIL!

In the "switching," parents are tempted to make voice mail out of their children, asking them to relay messages about child support payments, the needed repairs on the house, or comments about the other parent's new girlfriend or boyfriend. Such unreasonable demands and pressures make life unnecessarily difficult for children.

> "When my parents fought at home, I'd often be told, 'Tell your father that I . . .' and I'd politely decline after years of being yelled at for the message I delivered. Did it end when they divorced? No! Now it seems they forget they have e-mail, United States Postal Service, cell phones, and land lines to use for communication. The kid-communication line is out of service. What am I supposed to say when Dad asks, 'Now what in the **** did your stupid mother mean by that'?"

I'M NOT A CHILD ANYMORE

Children of parents who separate are often immediately expected to give up what parents consider their "childish" ways and take on adult responsibilities such as housework and child care. While there's nothing wrong with teaching children household chores, no child should have to be the "little man" or "little woman" of the house; especially when there are *two* homes to keep clean instead of one. Perhaps you've heard, "But Dad, I do housework at Mom's all the time." It may be true.

I'M ON THE ROAD AGAIN

> "Every other week I pack up my things to get ready to visit Dad. I pack on Thursday night, so he can swing by school and pick me up. The three-hour

drive back home (my other home) takes time in Friday night traffic. The time change doesn't help either. [The life of a child who shuttles between parents has all the travel pressures of a businessperson on the road plus the extra emotional stressors.] Do I miss visiting Dad so I don't miss my stepbrother's birthday celebration? What if I can't get home for Mother's Day because of baseball practice?"

And what happens to children's commitments? Should they drop out of baseball? What if they're in the championship and they won't be able to participate because the time has come to go to the other parent's home? Boy Scouts, Girl Scouts, religious education, sports, speech, music participation and competitions, as well as neighborhood pick-up games all become more difficult when you are present only part of the time.

Constant launching and re-entry stresses young minds focused on things other than whether or not they've packed their homework, medicine, dress clothes for worship, good shoes, face mask for baseball, the card they made for Dad or Mom, and their favorite CDs. When does a child rest?

They are back on the road Sunday night. Have they packed their homework, medicine, dress clothes, good shoes, favorite CDs, iPod, and the face mask for baseball once again? How many more times will they do this in their lives? When will it be over?

IT'S NOT OVER UNTIL IT'S OVER!

Yogi Berra had it right: "It ain't over till it's over." He was talking about baseball games, but the children of the switching hour would agree with him. The switching hour experience does not end when the parents have established themselves in new locations. It doesn't end when the child is a teenager. Shuttling between parents doesn't end when the child is eighteen or turns twenty-one. It doesn't end when they are young adults. It doesn't end when they are parents or grandparents themselves. The divided life continues as long as there are two parents who live in two separate homes and who both want a relationship with their children. It continues as long as the child travels between the two parental homes. As long as two parents live, there is a switching hour life. It is not over, until it's over.

The Switching Hour

Goodbys always make my throat hurt . . .
I need more hellos . . .
— Charles M. Schulz, Peanuts:
    © United Feature Syndicate, Inc.

CHAPTER TWO

THE HOUR I WAIT
AND LONG FOR

Dear Mom,

Finally made it—I waited for Dad at the airport for 3 hours! He ~~forgot~~ that I was arriving today. The job he's doing is so ~~demanding~~ He says he loves me and is glad I'm here.

Please take care of Socks for me this summer. You know rabbits don't sweat.

Give the "Steps" love from me. Tell them I've counted my CDs and they better be there when I get home in Aug.

Gosh Mom, I'm missing you so much already and have months to go. Make sure you give my friends my new number and the email address.. Forget the email, sorry, Dad said it was too expensive and that I should be doing better things with my time.

Hi to George.

All my love,

A.

USA 26

ZIP + 4.

UNITED STATES POSTAL SERVICE.

DOES TIME SLOW DOWN?

Recall how slowly time seems to move when you are waiting for a long-overdue vacation. Each day expands and the clock takes on the pace of an elephant—slow and deliberate. You might even check to see if your clock is still working. Remember how you counted down the days before school would be out. Five, four, three, two, one—FREEDOM!

Children of the switching hour mark time. They regularly count down weeks, days, hours, and minutes. How many days until I see Daddy? More than three? How many weeks before I see you again? What time did Mom say she'd meet us? I hope she's on time; I don't want to wait.

THE HOUR I WAIT AND LONG FOR

Waiting is what the children of the switching hour do. They wait to see the parent that they are not with, they wait to see siblings they've missed, they wait to see friends they've left, they wait to be a citizen of one world, and they wait to be in charge of deciding when they'll visit their parents.

And they wait in restaurants, parked cars, in airports, at the grandparents, at school or daycare, and at supervised visitation and transition sites for the switching to take place. As anyone who is prone to run late or is a stickler for being on time knows: *time matters*. When the clock pushes past the appointed hour, pressure starts to build, nerves tighten. The questions and worries begin. Is the parent being as careless as ever? Did they leave late yet again? Maybe the traffic's bad. Maybe there's an accident. Maybe they forgot.

"My precious moments of together time are ticking away. A Friday night movie won't work. Waiting to eat pizza with Mom was a bad idea; she's late and I'm starving. I'm exhausted from studying for my last exam and packing. Please Mom, hurry up. I think I'll sleep in this chair."

I CAN'T WAIT TO SEE MY OTHER PARENT

"Waiting is hard. I mark my calendar with an X each day and mark the target in bright pink. It reminds me of when I waited for Santa Claus and Christmas. Each day brought me closer to the end of the wait.

"June is a long wait when you start in January. Dad had business trips when I had breaks, and I had gymnastic events when he was home. I wonder what my room could look like at his house. He said we'd redecorate so I will feel more comfortable. The navy blue does nothing for my mood. Wish Mom could be here; she's great at fixing rooms so they just fit us.

"There's so much to tell Dad about—he hasn't heard about my latest boyfriend, my essay award, and my awful argument with my best friend. I wonder what dating was like for Dad or did he ever fight with his best friend?"

Waiting to see the other parent distances a child from life as he or she is living it. Living in two worlds also creates a sense of being distracted. What's going on in the other world? How is Mom? How's Dad's health? Is the stepparent treating my parent okay? Would Dad be mad if he knew I really like my stepdad? As the time for the transition between parents approaches, children may withdraw their attention from what is currently happening in anticipation of seeing the other parent. Or perhaps they act like they aren't going to leave at all.

What about the parent they're with? This is the dilemma of children who live in two worlds. When they've waited impatiently to see one parent, they have no sooner arrived than they start to miss the other parent. The younger the child, the more difficult it is for them to hold in their mind the image of the other parent; "seeing *is* believing" for a child who is little. Until children are three to five years old, the ability to know the parent still exists if they can't see them is not well developed. A young child who is left with one parent is immediately lonesome, sometimes beyond consolation.

I CAN'T WAIT TO SEE MY STEPBROTHERS AND HALF SISTERS

> "I miss Juan. We share a room at Mom's. He's my big brother and protector. If the monsters scare me, he says he'll beat them up. Why can't Juan come with me? He likes to fish and camp. Mom said he's visiting his dad when I'm visiting mine. Too bad."

—OR—

"I wish Janelle was here to help me with summer school. She knows this biology stuff inside and out. (Hey, she'd get the pun.) I told her she should be a doctor when she grows up. She smiles and asks me about where I'm stuck. She's with her father on a trip to Alaska. Some people have all the luck."

Sisters and brothers—step, half, and full—matter. Their acceptance or rejection shapes life in a powerful way, whether they're present in the household or not.

"I always wanted Becky to like me. She was so much older, but we shared the distinction of having red hair like our mother. She lived out West, so I never saw her much; but I thought about her often. She was my mother's oldest daughter. How could she live so far away?"

Family is family for a child. Young children do not understand the conflicts that arise about which child is under which parent's authority. For them, when it comes to power, you're either a parent or a child. They like the company of their siblings, and they want to be with them, especially when life is exciting or scary. There's strength in numbers.

I CAN'T WAIT TO SEE MY FRIENDS AGAIN

"I can't wait to see my best buds, my most beautiful girl, and reclaim my role as reigning champ of *Dance, Dance Revolution* (DDR game). I like to imagine that I push the pause button, like on the

DVD machine, when I walk out the door for the summer. Life will resume when I walk back in later. But life has no pause button. My best friend's moving next week. The girl I thought was hot and liked me (so her great e-mails and all the hours on the phone said) couldn't be without an 'on-site' boyfriend all summer now that she's sixteen. I'm a stranger in this life. How did that happen?"

On the other hand, there are friends who remain and who are loyal year in and year out. They weather the separations from their friends with a switching hour way of life.

"Shelly is great. When I'm gone she keeps notes on all the best gossip. She takes pictures and e-mails them to me. When the cheerleading coach wanted to start practice early, she spoke up and reminded her that I couldn't get back until the date we had agreed upon in the spring when I left. That's a friend for you. What would I do without Shelly? She stops by Mom's business and then tells me how she's *really* doing. Mom always tells Shelly what she keeps from me 'so I won't be upset so far away'."

The more involved children are in their schools, places of worship, work, and community, the more challenging a two-world life becomes. Will an employer replace them if they can't work certain weekends? What if the charity event they've been working on is scheduled for a weekend that is their weekend out of town with the other parent? What about sports, cheerleading, and band events that take place on

Friday nights or on the weekends when they are committed to being with the other parent? Will the rabbi, priest, imam, or minister consider them faithful if they miss half the time?

I CAN'T WAIT TO BE A CITIZEN OF ONE WORLD

When parents no longer live in the same home, it is as though the move destroys one world and creates two more. Everything that has been familiar and dependable, even the bad, changes. Routines and rituals are disrupted.

"Dad isn't here to cook every Monday, Wednesday, and Friday. Who will take Roxie to ballet when Mom has to work late? Alice is now doing the laundry because Mom's just too tired after her second job at night. No one has time for bedtime stories. Homework after supper is a 'do-it-yourself' project now. Dad always helped with schoolwork while Mom cleaned up the kitchen. What will we do on Sunday nights? Popcorn and board games aren't the same without Dad. You know he loved to win. Making popcorn is his specialty. He took his big popcorn machine with him, too. Wow, all these changes! My friend Maria's dad speaks only Spanish since he left the house. The U.S. ways destroyed his family, he believes. So, therefore, no English."

Routines and rituals give a sense of support, security, continuity, and safety. The familiar words and actions create space for the new, soothing us when upset and reminding us of the past—leading us to the future.

Here's a challenge. Try mixing up *your* morning routine. If you eat breakfast at home, eat at a drive-thru. If coffee and the paper begin your day, skip coffee and wait until evening to read your paper. You'll probably feel as though the rhythm of your day is upset. You may be a little cranky. A child likes routine as well.

Changes in a child's routine create crankiness in him or her, too. For children to have a sense that the two worlds have more than a little in common, they need similar patterns of eating, sleeping, affection, and discipline. Will this new world support life as he or she knows it? When children have to climb out of bed, rummage for anything that looks like food, and entertain themselves until nearly noon with the TV remote, the world is not hospitable to their needs.

"I can't wait until I have one house to call *my* home. All these famous folks with many houses can have them. I want all my stuff in one place. When I'm with Dad I think of a book I want to read—it's at Mom's. At Mom's there's a CD of Dad's I want to hear. Now home is where each of my parents live. I want to belong in one place. I want one address. I want one place to call home.

"Right now I live half in one world and half in the other. Do you think this could make me crazy? Schizo or something? Maybe I'll have multiple personalities. Dad likes me when I'm energized and peppy. We go golfing, boating, sailing, hiking, and skiing. We're always on the go. Before Mom's accident, Dad said she was just like me.

She was energized and did everything he did and more. That all changed.

"Mom is happy when I'm quiet. She's at the computer writing her book, so she wants me to read or to even take up quilting (her favorite hobby). No dancing around the living room to my wild music. Headphones were created for times like these. My own world will not be quiet."

I CAN'T WAIT UNTIL I CAN DECIDE WHEN I'LL VISIT EACH PARENT

The years of required switching hours will end. Enforced visitation will cease. Then the child, now a young adult, will decide when to visit his or her parents.

"I look forward to deciding when to visit each of my parents. I will love being able to visit Mom in the summer and see the flowerbeds. Each year I've missed their peak beauty. Visiting Dad on his birthday in late December will no longer involve negotiating Christmas vacation so I can see him when 'it's not his year' to have me between Christmas and New Year's.

"I will feel as free as a kid whose braces have just been removed.

"I will rejoice in being able to come and go when I choose.

"I will not miss racing down the road to meet the other parent for the exchange of me and my belongings (why do you need all this stuff?!), which invariably takes longer than it should, because there was always something: 'terrible traffic . . . no gas in the car . . . couldn't find the keys . . . Mary hadn't brought the car back from art supply shopping on time, we had to pick up your half sister Mindy from her work making evergreen Christmas decorations, then we had to go and find Randi, your stepsister, in the elementary school helping her teacher grade papers because her mother, Linda Jo, was still working at the light store. Yes, we forgot you said you wanted to meet us earlier than the usual time'!

"I'VE HEARD IT ALL—I can't wait until it's over.

"I will not miss feeling guilty if I'm eager to go home . . . it will be my home, not the residence of the other parent.

"I will not miss being lonesome for the kids who belong in the house, but who are off visiting their other parent during so many of my stays. I can't wait for the last switching hour to come. Dad tells me, 'Don't wish your life away.' Maybe I am."

The Switching Hour

Love reckons hours for months, and days for years; and every little absence is an age.
—John Dryden

CHAPTER THREE

THE HOUR I HOPE COMES, BUT DOES NOT

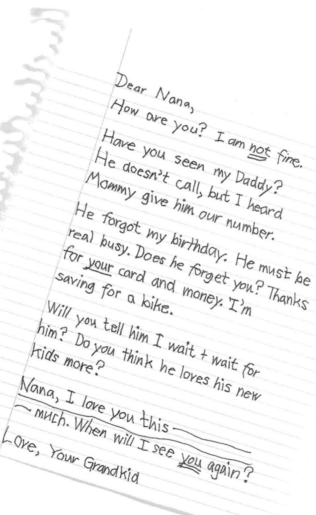

Dear Nana,

How are you? I am not fine.

Have you seen my Daddy? He doesn't call, but I heard Mommy give him our number.

He forgot my birthday. He must be real busy. Does he forget you? Thanks for your card and money. I'm saving for a bike.

Will you tell him I wait + wait for him? Do you think he loves his new kids more?

Nana, I love you this much. When will I see you again?

Love, Your Grandkid

WHEN TIME HASN'T HELPED

How many times have you heard in the midst of some of your worst moments in life, "Give it time. Time will heal this. Just hang in there." Your well-meaning friends are often right—the car gets fixed, your surgery scars fade, and you find a new love in your life. But what happens when time doesn't help? When the problems do not shrink over time? That is what it is like for a child to hope against all odds.

THE HOUR THAT DOES NOT COME

Children are great optimists. They are full of hope. "Maybe when Daddy isn't so sad about the divorce, he'll call for me. When Daddy starts paying the child support, maybe Mom won't have to work so much. If I'm older, Dad will want to spend time with me." Days and years pass. And they hope.

I'M HOPING DADDY COMES TO SEE ME OR ASKS ME TO VISIT

"I was five when Daddy left. He was too far away to see me, he said, but he called and talked every now and then. For a couple of years I had birthday presents. Daddy saw me one Christmas and then it stopped. Doesn't he know how much I miss him? I want him to teach me football. I think he'll like me more. Dad was a great player. He left his college trophies here. Mom threw them in the trash, yelling 'He cared more about that (can't say it) football than he ever cared about us. What did he ever do half the year but sit, watch football with his wild friends, and drink?' I didn't know I'd get a lecture about Daddy and football; I just want to learn to play. The son of the greatest football player on the university team of . . . can't remember the year . . . ought to know how to play football. Maybe my uncle will teach me. Dad said they were a real kick (can't say it) pair those two. Doesn't my Daddy think of me? Does he have a new son? I'll always be his first kid. That should count for something."

Over half of the children of divorce are begging for their fathers to come and see them. They wait for fathers and mothers to ask to see them, to call, write, send an e-mail, anything. Have they been forgotten? They long for a switching hour that does not come.

"I guess we are a 'throw away' family, just like those paper plates we use all the time so Mama doesn't have to do dishes. Pa was so loving and kind. He helped us with our homework. Pa even *said* he loved us and everything. But he left us when I had just turned eleven. Walked out in the midst of a fight with Mama about . . . what was it . . . oh yeah, something about all the money he was spending fixing up his 'classic' Mustang. Well, he got into that classic car and left us, his 'throw away' family, behind. He never came back. Just slammed the door so hard the glass broke—it still is—and squealed the precious tires on his classic car and left.

"Guess it was all lies. All those sweet things he used to tell me. 'You're going to be the prettiest girl in high school,' and 'No matter how old you are you'll always be my little girl.' High school is over and he still doesn't know if I'm pretty or not. I guess I still am his little girl."

Children waiting for time with both parents ask, "Where are you, Dad?" "Why don't you want to see me, Mom?" Your children do not care about your success or lack of it. They don't care about how much money you make. However, life is much easier for them when you pay your child support on time. What they care about is YOU. You are important, no matter how you feel about yourself or the other parent. Your kids still wait and hope as each birthday and holiday approaches. They don't want to hear excuses. They dream, "Maybe this is the year I'll hear from Daddy." "This birthday Mom will ask me to come to her home to see her."

You are not disposable. You are not replaceable. You are one of the pair of suns around which the hearts of your children rotate. It doesn't matter if they are five, fifteen, or fifty; kids want to know they are important to the people they call parents.

I'M HOPING MY PARENT WILL GROW UP

"Dad has just never grown up. When I was little, he played Nintendo all day, partied all night, and slept until after noon. My Grandma said that he'd grow out of it, that he was just making up for the time he lost by being trapped into parenthood so young. I didn't understand that trapped part.

"But here's my dad's picture. I know it's the back of his head, but it's the part that I always see when I'm with him, even today. He isn't playing Nintendo now; he's working on the computer. Says he can work at home as well as in the office with all this modern technology. If the computer and fax are available, he's 'good to go' according to him. Trading stocks must be quite an easy job, 'cause after an hour or so, he's doing other things. He doesn't know I sneak in behind him to see if he's still working. If seeing all those naked people is part of his work, I'll bet his boss doesn't know. The stuff that pops up when I'm trying to e-mail Mom is gross. Makes me feel creepy and dirty just having to click the delete button on it. I don't think he knows I check the history on his computer. Boy, no wonder he says he's poor, the stuff he's paying to see! I hope he doesn't expect me to like seeing this stuff when he wants guy time when I'm older. It's disgusting. I turn over all his magazines on the coffee table and cover them with something respectable. I thought he'd change when he grew up, whenever that is. Grandma was wrong about Dad."

Children often think that divorce will change their parents. They will be better, more attentive, more responsible, more loving now that the divorce is over and they say they are happier. But, unfortunately, that is often not the case. Children often assume that because a parent says he or she is happier, the relationship with the child will be better. Children of the switching hour wish for the day when their parents turn their attention to their children and really see them. The children want to be listened to, talked to, and appreciated for who they are. They want time with you. They want to *share* time with you.

"Mom always promised me time—just girl time, the two of us doing something fun, something you want to do. Not some tag-along grown-up thing like watching her shop, get her hair done, or the super boring manicure and pedicure routine. Her excuses for spending endless hours doing her errands and projects are always the same: 'There's just not enough time during the week to get all these things in. I know, honey, you're only here every other weekend, but I fly to see Joseph when you aren't here. You know he has such a busy schedule and really isn't the kid-type. Yes, I could have shopped during the week, but you know they run such fabulous sales on the weekends.' On and on . . .

"When I was little she'd get babysitters for me during the weeks I spent with her and just when I thought I'd get to see her for the weekend, we'd drive off to the grandparents so they could 'see their precious grandchild.' If I was so precious, why wasn't she ever around? Just as well. Grandpa and Grandma are extra nice to me. They feel bad for me too, but don't dare say much because Mom will throw a cussing, ranting fit and no one needs that."

I'M HOPING MY PARENT WILL LIKE ME

After a breakup, the adults want to forget about the person with whom they had the relationship. If they mutually wanted it to end, that is. If not, it's like they can't let go of a live electric wire. In either situation, for the children of the switching hour, if they remind the parent they're visiting of the one who has been left, it brings pain. Now the sarcastic, "You're just like your mother," or "You're a clone of your dad" is a blow to a child's self-esteem!

"I think my dad just doesn't like women and girls. He believes that we are second-class citizens who belong in the home. My sisters and I should be doing the housework and raising children. That's it. My desire to go to college and become a child psychiatrist doesn't please him at all. He considers the education of women to be a waste of time. I love school, am a straight *A* student, and plan to go to UCLA. He does not care. Dad believes that if the **** feminists hadn't gotten my mother stirred up, his life would still be great.

"It's a little hard to understand, really. His mom was a country schoolteacher and helped his father run the family farm. She was the brains of the operation, if the truth be told.

"Doesn't help that I look just like Mom when he met her. I found an old photo album of the two of them when I was visiting my grandparents. Looking at her was just like looking at me. If he could just tell me that, I'd feel better. Instead he keeps harping about how much smarter boys are, and how I better pay attention to my weight or no man will want me. I love my father, but visiting him for the summer depresses me until Thanksgiving."

Children are loyal to both parents. Yes, there are reasons you decided the relationship couldn't work anymore. Remember that while you were able to distance yourself from whatever upset you the most about your former significant other, your child still lives in the world between the two of you whether you were together for one year or twenty-five. A child loves his or her parents no matter what.

"Mom still thinks I am betraying her when I spend time with Dad. I know he hasn't stopped drinking despite the thousands of promises. Yes, he gets depressed and stays in his room for days. During those days, I watch television, read, and wait for him to come out to go to the bathroom so I can say 'Hi.' I worry about Dad. That last attempt to fix his life by ending it almost worked. Thank God he was so drunk he didn't realize the tank was near empty and the car ran out of gas!

"The Iraq War wrecked him. I don't know what happened, but he screams at night and mumbles about having killed women and children by mistake. I miss the Dad I knew before. Tell the people in government that the families fight wars without medals, without compensation, without relief. There, Dad's crying again. Wonder what he's thinking about now.

"Mom says tough love is the way to go with Dad. No sobriety, no visits.

"I want to be tough, but my heart is tender."

I'M HOPING MY PARENTS WILL BE OVER THE DIVORCE

Recovery from a breakup or a divorce takes time, even if it was seen as being necessary and the right thing to do by both parties. If there is disagreement and dissent, however, with one party refusing to agree that the decision is the right one, the children often receive the anger and misery of the parent who was opposed to changing the relationship.

"All the verbs in my mother's house are past tense. On and on she goes, 'I used to have a good life. Our house was the largest and most well furnished in the subdivision. I could always count on Eloise to keep it immaculate. And the meals she cooked, they were exquisite! I used to belong to the country club. I used to be able to buy a new car every two years. When your dad and I were married, we went scuba diving twice a year. When I put your dad through law school, he told me he'd never forget how hard I was working for us. 'Us'—what a concept. He wouldn't know 'us' if it bit him in the butt.

" 'When we were married, you kids didn't have to worry about money for college. Remember the pool parties I planned for you and your little friends? Parties—remember all those cocktail parties that I hosted with your dad? "Good for business," he'd say. I thought whatever was good for his practice, would be good for all of us, so parties and more parties it was.

" ' "Don't worry," your dad would say, "I won't do anything so cliché as having an affair with the secretary." Boy, he was right. His new junior partner fit that bill. The money was better, too. Yes, I used to be thin and blond. Wonder if she knows she'll face a trade in her future when she's no longer such great eye candy. You go look in my closet and see the great clothes I used to wear. G*d, I used to be in fabulous shape.'

"Sometimes I don't think mom knows I'm in the room anymore when she starts in. I *want* to tell her that I'm sorry that her—our—great life is over, but please, can we live in the now. I don't. She'd be mad. Sometimes she puts that two-caret diamond ring back on her left hand and spends the whole week telling us how Dad will realize his mistake and be begging to come back any day now. I'm telling you, it won't happen. Would I like it to happen? Yes, I'd love my—our—old life back. But, it won't happen. I know that. But on and on she goes."

The Switching Hour

Absence from whom we love
    is worse than death,
and frustrate[s] hope severer than despair.
—William Cowper, "On Her Endeavouring to Conceal Her
  Grief at Parting"

CHAPTER FOUR

THE HOUR I WISH WOULDN'T COME

Dear Dad,

Help me, please!! Mom is at it again. She isn't taking her meds, so she doesn't ever sleep at night. Her drinking is WORSE!

Her yelling doesn't end—and—she bugs me about you and your new life/wife CONSTANTLY!

And— ALL THE GUYS — I am so tired of all her new boyfriends. Each is worse than the last. I can't take it, Dad.

Will you please come and get me, please— please? I promise I won't beg to live with Mom again. I just worry about her when I'm with you. What if she has a car wreck when she drives drunk and hurts one of the kids when she's in the mood to "discipline" us? I keep wondering about the other kids. Will you talk to their dad?

I can't help her Dad. I try & clean the house, and take care of the other kids so she isn't so MAD all the time.

I don't want to come back here, Dad. Please e-mail me soon! Don't call. Mom will know something's wrong. Please,

Love — Z

WISHING MY LIFE AWAY

C hildren of the switching hour wish their lives were different. They wish there weren't more switching hours to come—more than they can count.

They wish their parents *would not* marry, or divorce, again. Sometimes they wish a parent *would* marry or would divorce again. They wish they knew what their families were going to be like. They ask: Will I have stepbrothers and stepsisters? Will I have more half siblings?

They wish they didn't have to visit parents and step-parents who are difficult.

They wish holidays would not come.

And they wish they didn't have to say good-bye and leave once again.

I WISH THE SWITCHING HOUR WOULDN'T COME

"It's the switching that keeps me always on edge. I just get comfortable, and then it's time to go. It takes me awhile to adjust to being at Mom's with all the other kids (my half siblings). The noise level is so intense . . . all the toys and chaos. I am sure they own every toy I've seen advertised on Saturday mornings during cartoon time. When I'm there, I keep my stuff in my suitcase because I can never find it when we're hurrying to get ready to leave so I can meet Dad. I also am able to lock my suitcase. I have to keep my cell phone there 'cause the little kids love to use it to talk to each other when they're playing. I still owe Dad for one bill they ran up when I wasn't paying attention!

"This is so different from my dad's place. He's got the basics and that's it. Here, Mom keeps the place filled with her golf gear, camping equipment, and computers. She must have six of them when you count the laptops. Dad just watches sports. She asks me to golf with her, but while I know all about golf, I resist the offer since I am quite a poor golfer because I only play golf with her! Dad won't pay for it!

"Anyway, I was saying, I just get adjusted, and then it's time to head back to Dad's. I don't think either Mom or Dad know this, but I have always felt so much stress (yes, kids get stressed) and pressure when it's time to switch. My stomach hurts and sometimes my head does too. Should I eat before I leave Mom's? Will Dad want me to eat with him as soon as I see him? I don't ever guess correctly.

"As I prepare for switching hour number five hundred (some people count home runs, I count switches), I have some questions I'd love to ask *both* my parents. These are *questions* that bug me all the time . . ."

Will you be there?

"Do you have any idea what it's like to sit in the car at McDonald's and wait? Waiting inside isn't any better. After I've eaten, they expect me to leave, not sit and warm a booth for another hour. Yes, you wait for planes all the time, but this is different. When I was little, I was sure you'd forgotten me when you were late. Remember those times you *did* forget?

"Mom would be getting madder and madder, because the other kids needed to do their homework or to be bathed and put to bed, but here she was waiting with me 'yet again.' Yes, we wait for her, too, but she says you don't have anyone else to worry about, so no big deal if you have to wait. The TiVo will take care of all that matters to you.

"I have always felt like such a burden to both of you during the switching—such a pain in your day."

Will you be glad to see me or mad because you had to drive?

"Every week I worry about your moods. I pray that traffic is fine and that you will not be in an accident. The construction has been a nightmare for you, I know. I just want you to be glad to be with me."

Will you argue about me or something else?

"It is more than obvious to me that you two don't belong together, but do you think you could stop arguing every time you drop me off or pick me up? If I have managed not to get a headache before, I feel quite sick by the time you've yelled about his share of the summer camp bill for the umpteenth time. Let it go!

"Please don't discuss whether or not I'm still grounded the minute you pick me up. Dad feels that you, Mom, are too strict. You worry that I'll turn into a criminal like you claim Dad is. You remind me that white-collar crime is the same as robbing a bank. You know what happens to bank robbers.

"I feel like that unpaid bill that's tossed between the two of you. 'Here, you take care of it.' 'No, you deal with it.' "

Will either of you have someone new with you in the car for me to meet?

"How would you like to meet a person who could possibly be your new 'parent' without any warning? I feel trapped when you have someone new with you. I'm not ready for the small talk. I miss your last partner, too. What is happening? There's someone new every week. I just don't have enough energy to be fun after being at Mom's. I'm sad for her, for the kids, and for the babies. I'm wondering if I remembered all my books, DVDs, and CDs. I'm exhausted because the twins aren't sleeping through the night. I try to give Mom a break taking care of the babies at night when I'm there, since Dopey left her once the twins came."

Why can't you just get back together and make this stop?

"You haven't found anyone else you like. You still argue with each other, just the same as always. Why can't this be over? Dad could be back in the house tonight. Think of all the extra time I would have in my life without all this travel. I wouldn't have to fly to Holland to be with the grandparents

when Dad can't keep me all summer. Please, can't
you just get back together?"

I WISH THINGS WOULD NOT CHANGE AT MOMMY'S OR AT DADDY'S

The relationships of the children of the switching hour are
filled with an overwhelming amount of change. Not only do
the relationships with each parent change, but the relationships with their parents' significant others and their children
also are sources of joy and pain in a child's life. They are
expected to smile, be quiet, and to adapt.

> "I don't know who will be at Daddy's. Maybe his
> girlfriend and her kids. Maybe his best friend and
> his son will be there all weekend. And sometimes,
> it's just Daddy and me. I like that best. I want to
> be with him, 'cause I miss him all the time.

> "Mommy said that I should be excited. I'm going
> to be having a new brother. She and my stepdaddy
> are having a baby boy soon. I said I didn't want
> another new brother, but she hit me hard."

Happiness in the lives of the parents does not always
equal happiness in the lives of their children. Researchers
have found that "trickle down" happiness doesn't work
(Judith S. Wallerstein, Julia M. Lewis, and Sandra Blakeslee,
The Unexpected Legacy of Divorce: A 25 Year Landmark Study
[New York: Hyperion, 2000], xxix).

> "The dates of my parents' second marriages are
> days that mark the beginning of new dreams for

them and the end of an old dream for me. I always hoped that my parents would get back together; even when one of them had remarried, I believed that all that stood between that and my parents' remarriage was a divorce. Since I knew that was possible, I was hopeful for years. I guess I should be glad that my dad is happily married. It was when my mom got remarried that I knew my dream of their remarriage was merely a fantasy. Those were hours I wished wouldn't come. I must be wishing on the wrong star."

In addition to changes in the adult relationships in their lives, children of the switching hour experience frequent changes in their sibling structures. The position we hold in our family is significant for our personality development. Imagine moving from being the oldest in your family to being in the middle overnight.

"I have been an only child, an oldest child, and a middle child. When my parents were living together (they never married), I was an only. When my mother married when I was six, I became the oldest of four (three stepsisters). Their mom had died, so Mom adopted them.

"I was the youngest for the short time Dad was married to the band director of my school whose daughter is one year older than I. That divorce made my life messy 'til I was out of middle school.

"My dad just remarried. After being his only child, I have now become a middle child at age fourteen! His new partner's son and daughter are seven and seventeen, respectively. I had thought having an older sister again would be fun, but she was used to being the only girl, or shall I say princess, so having a thinner, smarter sister isn't her idea of a good time. I wonder if her mother knows that she binges in the middle of the night. And having a brother—finally!—is great. BUT— why is he already asking me about sex, I wonder?

"As you can see, I have several different families. So when someone asks me where I am in the family, I have to ask them which family they're talking about."

I WISH THE HOUR OF VISITING MY TROUBLED FAMILY WOULDN'T COME

Remember there were reasons why you are no longer with your child's other parent. The list of reasons for leaving a lover keeps songwriters in business: lying, cheating, drinking, drugs, pornography, compulsive shopping and spending, miserliness, no sexual interest, sexual obsession, gun obsession, Internet or TV addiction, laziness, joblessness, overworking, degree obsession, no interest in education, messiness, cleanliness, being a religious nut, lack of interest in spirituality, sports addiction, criminal behavior, violence, abusive language, mental illness, inability to grow up, and more. The list includes irritations that are intolerable as well as behaviors that are dangerous and deadly. There was enough trouble in the relationship for you to decide to end it. Your children, however, live between the two of you still. They are not able to end it. The two of you will always be his or her parents. There is no reason to think that the moods, words, and behaviors that hurt and troubled you will not also hurt and trouble your child.

It is your responsibility to protect your children. Check out what they tell you when they report behavior that may sound outrageous to you, particularly if there are a lot of people you do not know in your former significant other's life and home.

"I didn't want to visit my daddy and his new girl-friend ever again. But Mommy said the law said I had to go. Daddy would be sad if I didn't go to see him.

"The plane ride was bad. We kept hitting bumps in the sky, kinda like the ones we speed over in the parking lots and the car scrapes. The big people kept shouting and asking God to help them.

"The airplane lady asked, 'Are you really five years old? You're the smallest five we've had this summer.' Mommy always says I should eat more. But my tummy always hurts.

"Daddy's friends are creepy. They sit and smoke something that smells funny. Daddy drinks and drinks something my friends call 'icky drink.' Then he goes to sleep.

"I'm so scared in the dark. I have a Minnie Mouse nightlight at Mommy's, but Daddy says I should just grow up, G*dd**n kids! In the dark somebody touches me down there. I don't know who it is. I can't breathe. I think I'm going to die. Mommy doesn't believe me when I tell her. She thinks I'm having bad dreams in the dark.

"I know Daddy will hit me when he sees I've wet the bed again. I try to stay awake all night, but I can't. The bathroom is in Daddy's room. His girlfriend said I should keep my *** out of there."

Sometimes it is a parent that a child doesn't want to visit. For others it is the stepparent or the significant other who lives with a parent they love that causes them suffering.

"My father's new wife, who informed me never to refer to her as stepmother, detested me from the beginning. I guess it was because I knew about the two of them from the start of their little romance and told my mother all about it.

"My father takes me with him on all his trips. I have great vision, an excellent memory for details, and I'm thoroughly trained in organization by my very particular mother. On the other hand, my father has always had poor eyesight and so much attention deficit disorder, it is a wonder he ever finishes any film he starts. (I find it ironic that he so values organization in me, but divorced my mother because 'her orderliness squelched his creativity.' From this vantage point, the only squelching she did was to ask him to give up his constant philandering, which he absolutely refused to do. Crassly stated, he likes women, lots of them.)

"Anyway, back to my point, my father's wife makes sure that he and I have virtually no time for just the two of us. If I suggest a restaurant or a movie, she'll enthusiastically exclaim that 'she'd love to join us.' Join us, right, she's worried Father might ask about Mother or give me some extra money, not that *she* goes without anything. It's a good thing Father's family had money. She's making sure wealth won't be a multigenerational problem.

"Any remarks that my father reports from his current wife about me are negative. I'm not friendly enough to her. I don't compliment her on her clothes. I don't report that I've seen the two of them in the latest magazine when Father received an award for his last documentary. I tell him I am exhausted with the 'playing nice' game and would love to be able to be real around him once again. I want the sweatshirt and blue jean days again. I'm sick of designer clothes and the hottest hairstyle the movie stylists come up with. I don't want to compete with her. For heaven's sake, she's nearly fifty and I'm seventeen."

I WISH THE HOLIDAYS WOULDN'T COME

Don't sign your child up for the Scrooge award just because they're down on the holidays. Holidays bring with them an expectation of fun, joy, relaxation, play, happiness, laughter, and lots of digital camera moments. Holidays are to be eagerly awaited, we say.

However, let's look at the holidays from the perspective of the children of the switching hour. Not only do they have expectations of family togetherness on holidays, they anticipate more intense family separation and conflict at the holidays as well. It is usually only possible to spend Christmas Eve with one parent and maybe Christmas Day with the other, assuming they live near each other. If the distances are great or holiday plans complicated, then the child may not be able to be with one parent (and perhaps a stepparent and other siblings—half, full, or step) for at least part of the celebration. If the Parenting Plan or court order states that there will be every other year holiday celebrations, the sense of continuity in the holidays is lost. Last year's pictures may not necessarily bring happy memories.

Even longer celebrations such as Hanukkah may require a child to miss something significant in one or the other parent's household. A special Passover celebration may be discussed for years, always reminding the children that they missed it in their shuttle between the two worlds. Kwanzaa may not be celebrated in one parent's home. Ramadan observation becomes nearly impossible if both parents do not share the same religion.

For many, holiday celebrations involve traveling long distances in bad weather. Snowstorms have stalled more than cars, trucks, planes, and trains. A long-awaited reunion with a nonresidential parent may have to be canceled because of the weather. The relationship is put on hold. No memory building this holiday.

Children of the switching hour learn not to hope too much. They learn to "wait and see." If they don't hope and plan, there's less to be disappointed about.

"I remember when I stopped believing in Santa Claus. I asked him to please let me see both parents on my seventh Christmas. My dad had left before Christmas the year before and we didn't know where he was until the last day of the year. I just wanted to be with them both on my favorite day.

"I started counting down the days until Christmas on Halloween. I was glad when Christmas decorations were mixed in with the leftover masks and unsold candy corn. Pretty soon, I'd have a wonderful time with *both* parents. You see, they were great at creating a fairyland around our house—inside and out. The decorations were everywhere. Some of my best memories are of helping Dad untangle the lights. Mom and Dad would stay up late with Christmas music cranked up loud. Mom and I baked and decorated cookies. Cutout sugar cookies, decorated with colored frosting, were my specialty. For once, no mention was made of my bedtime.

"Then, it was over. On my sixth Christmas there were no lights, no decorations, and no pretty sugar cookies. Dad gave us our presents after Christmas. It was on New Year's Day; we watched him watch football all day on his new big-screen TV."

I WISH THE HOUR FOR ME TO LEAVE WOULDN'T COME

A child may be upset with the prospect of leaving. He or she may find all kinds of reasons to extend the stay: her best friend is having a pool party she doesn't want to miss; his friend's sister is coming home and she was his favorite babysitter; they'll beg you to let them stay another weekend; or the coolest neighbor, Matt, has asked them to go to the theme park with him for the weekend to ride that new roller coaster. All are events that a child enjoys and does not want to miss.

Most often they do not want to leave because they will miss you. It does not necessarily mean that there's something wrong in the other home. Leaving is difficult for many people. It is especially difficult for a child who leaves a parent whom they love.

"Leaving is the worst. It's not because I'm not eager to see Mom. I've been missing her for two months now. It's just that I'm used to being here. I've been working with Dad on the shrimp boat. He calls her, 'My Delight.' Yeah, he's like a kid out there even though he's working like the devil. Life on the water is where I belong. Maybe this water thing is in our genes. Dad's dad was a shrimper, too. I'm so glad Dad decided that I was old enough, translate this 'big enough,' to be of some use to him this summer. He actually complimented me on some of my work. I'll never tie knots as easily as he does. Even the most complicated knot is as simple as tying his shoelaces for him.

"There's nothing prettier than a sunrise seen from the boat. Sure wish I could talk to Bubba of *Forrest Gump* fame. He'd understand my passion and sorrow at leaving this place for the hallowed halls of my private high school. The smells of furniture polish and floor wax as well as the academic hush will only serve to remind me of how much I miss the smell of the sea, the whip of the wind in the rigging, and the call of the gulls. Think I'll bring some sand and shells with me. They'll remind me that the ocean, shrimp, and Dad are waiting for me.

"Mom will not be pleased that I've come to love every aspect of the shrimp industry. Her expectations are that I will pursue my education and do something much more befitting of her family's name. Her political connections extend back to the Declaration of Independence. I think they should have had more children. Maybe then they'd each have a child to groom.

"So, today's my last day on the water for months. I'll leave all my clothes here. No place to use or store them at Mom's. Don't think she'd even let me have them in her house. I'll be at Mom's for a week; then it's off to school. Wonder what she's done to my room while I've been gone. Or who she's dating this time. Somebody big in business or politics. That much is a given.

"I am not ready for her world. I'll miss Dad so much. I'll miss the ocean, the beach house, working hard with my body, and all the quiet. I read every book on my summer reading list during the first two weeks, even though I have a hard time finishing my assignments at school. Too many distractions for me there. I even read Dad's history books. He knows all about World War II. Tells me I should pay attention to what went on then. It could happen again.

"My buddies weren't here, and Dad's computer leaves a lot to be desired. He says it works just fine for keeping track of his business. I helped him make a couple improvements with some newer software. He appreciated that and said that all that expensive education my grandparents are paying for is paying off. I didn't tell him I learned what I taught him in a public middle school! Tomorrow, courtesy of a short plane ride, it's back to my other world. Mom will be disgusted with how little I know about what's happening politically. I don't want to tell her that it all runs together for me."

The Switching Hour

Where is the good in good-bye?
—Meredith Willson, *The Music Man*

THE HOUR I TRY TO AVOID

To: betsy@email.com
Cc:

Subject: Wedding Plans . . .

▶ Attachments: *none*

Dear Betsy,
Funny you should ask about my wedding plans today on the phone. I'm emailing you so I won't cry.

After the horrible experience we had with my divorced parents at my brother's graduation, Sam and I have just decided to elope. There'll be no chance for the parents to fight like cats and dogs, ruining our happy day. You'd think they'd be beyond this type of stuff by now. Yes, they had 26 years, but it's over.

I worry that even though Sam and I are blissfully happy now, something dreadful like that might happen to us. I don't want my parents' life.

I'll miss you and know that I would love to have had you be a bridesmaid at my dream wedding, but at this point the "dream" has too much potential of being a "nightmare."

Stay in touch. I'll call you soon.
Love,
M.

LET'S NOT GO THERE

Children of the switching hour who move between the two worlds of their parents soon learn that there are situations and events to be avoided if at all possible. For some kids it means that they will never bring up the other parent, because any reference to that person results in a tirade.

For others, there will be conscious efforts to resist any attachments to the significant others that a parent brings into their lives. A child wonders, "Will this relationship end, too?"

THE HOUR I TRY TO AVOID

Tension builds when events arise that normally are celebrated with both extended families. Children will sometimes avoid attending an event such as a graduation just so their families won't gather. They will try to find a way around having their alienated parents in the same place at the same time.

And most importantly, children with divorced or alienated parents seek to avoid repeating the mistakes their parents made. Sometimes that means not making a marital commitment or having children.

I TRY TO AVOID ATTACKS ON MY OTHER PARENT

"I told Mommy, 'Daddy's got a new car in the garage. It's a real pretty green.' She got so mad. I heard about everything he had bought from the day they got married. There were large tools, boats, snowmobiles, motorcycles (I knew he loved Harleys—we always stop and look at the store—didn't know he's owned three), and lawn equipment for one of his 'hair-brained' business ventures (Mommy didn't like it when I asked her about 'hair-brained'). He was even going to make art. Hey, I like art. 'Check the garage for the stacks of colored glass,' she said, 'if you don't believe me. Do you know how expensive red glass is?'

"She yelled and yelled about credit cards. Then Mommy cried and said she hated going to bankruptcy court (don't know what that is). When she said Daddy didn't love me very much 'cause he didn't give her any money for me, I cried and cried. I told her that Daddy did love me, he told me he did. Mommy said Daddy always was good with the sugar. What does that mean? Sugar's bad for your teeth, Granny says. When Daddy buys something new, better not tell Mommy. She's on the phone screaming at Daddy right now. Then she'll go to her room. First she'll tell me to watch my videos and let her have some peace. I know all the words and songs to the videos 'cause this isn't the first time she's told me how bad Daddy is. He just loves his big boy toys. Why did I want to see him ever? He's my Daddy, I said. I hope she comes out for the phone so I can ask her for something to eat. Some days she stays in her pajamas all day and just comes out to feed me."

Trying to figure out their parents is part of what children do. They ask Dad about Mom and Mom about Dad. That way, they come to understand the feelings and behaviors of the other parent more quickly and thoroughly than if they are left to their own reflections. We all check out impressions of others. Kids are stunted in their emotional development if they learn that their questions about the other parent will *always* bring anger and negative comments. Children love even the cruelest and most abusive parents, even though they may wish their parents were different. The tragedy for these children is, for them, love will always involve great emotional and/or physical suffering.

I TRY TO AVOID LOVING MY STEPPARENTS AND THEIR FAMILIES

If you are a child of the switching hour whose parents have dated a lot or had several people who've lived with them, it may be hard to believe that this time the person (and often his or her children) will stay in your parent's life. If this happens in both parents' relationships at the same time, you may decide that keeping an emotional distance is the only safe thing to do. Visitation of parents is complicated enough. Are there stepparent visitation rights if the new marriage doesn't work?

"I didn't want to like my mom's new boyfriend.

He was so different from my father. Dad would

not be caught dead doing things that Mac seems to really enjoy doing with Mom. Do real men enjoy working with flowers and going to the symphony? Dad says an emphatic, 'No.' Dad has a liberal arts education, but you'd never know it. He considers doing that 'cushy' stuff a waste of time and a putting on of airs. Sad thing is, Dad is really talented musically, but is too macho to enjoy it very often. He'll only play if his friends bring their instruments by and beg for a couple of hours. After a few beers, he reaches under the bed, dusts off the case, and takes out his 'Delilah.' Yes, that's what he calls his fiddle. He says making music is his weakness, 'That d**n Nashville dream cost me twenty years of my life. Who would have thought that you could ruin country music? It went pop, and I stayed country!'

"Dad's idea of a good time is hunting, fishing, and just plain old hiking. He has taught me the names of all the birds, wildflowers, and trees that we've seen together. I studied his books for years. When I could identify all the birds, trees, or wildflowers that he pointed out (the ones he had taught me), then he'd buy me the guide. The field guides are some of my most prized gifts from him. I love our weeks in the cabin. The outdoor plumbing doesn't bother me one bit.

"Mac couldn't tell you one bird from another. He doesn't remember the trees in the front yard. I didn't want to like him. How would a guy raised in a big city understand a girl like me? Mac has taught me to love the violin. He said that since Dad is so musically talented and Mom, too, I probably would be good. He's right. I play the 'fiddle' when I'm with Dad and the 'violin' when I'm with Mom and Mac. Dad didn't know what to think when Mom and Mac bought me the violin when I turned twelve. He thought my mom had already spent enough time struggling to live one musician's dream (his) until it wrestled them both to a divorce. She surely wouldn't encourage *me* to love music.

"Mac isn't bitter like my dad. His dreams have come true. He is the CEO of a business his father started years ago. Mac always knew what he wanted to do and he's doing it. Guess Dad always knew what he wanted to do too, but the music people didn't see it his way. He said he got tired of always being the backup guy to those young hotshots. His line is, 'Always the bridesmaid and never the bride.' Kind of funny coming from him. Sad, too.

"I didn't want Mac and Mom to have any kids together. I had been my mother's only child for ten years and my grandmother's only grandchild. I liked life the way it was. Mac's kid moved in and he was the center of their attention. His son Jared was in his custody, so I shared my life every day with a four-year-old. He was such a baby.

"It was one thing to share Mom with Mac and Jared, but having a baby brother and sister was not on my list of life experiences *that I didn't want to miss.* Adults don't ask your permission. I really try to like Patrick and Monica, but I am still working on getting used to them. I didn't want to like them even though I'm sure if Mom and Mac divorced, the kids, except Jared of course, would be with us. After all, I've spent most of my life with Mom since she and Dad split. I don't like to be negative. Mac and Mom get along pretty well and have been together for seven years. Doesn't that seem like a long time? Still, she and Dad were together fifteen years, never fought, and yet one day Mom said we were going back home. I thought we *were* home."

I TRY TO AVOID HAVING MY ALIENATED PARENTS IN THE SAME PLACE

As any *Star Trek* fan knows, entertaining guests from different galaxies or worlds can prove quite challenging. Children of the switching hour face no lesser challenges.

So many of life's most significant moments take place within the gathering of extended family and friends. While one might plan two different Christmas celebrations or visits during Hanukkah, there is only one graduation, one wedding, one funeral, one reunion around which a family gathers. The purpose of these events has been to gather as a unit when one of the members of the family undergoes profound joy or sorrow. The strength, joy, and support are in the gathering. The surrounding of a beloved one with the wisdom and power of a community has existed through time.

What happens when the events no longer mean the anticipation of support, wisdom, continuity, and joy? What happens to a person when thinking about having both of his or her parents together is not the warm and cozy feeling of reassurance that a young child gets snuggling between both parents, protected on the right and left? An adult child of divorce recalls, "One of my strongest memories as a young child was my parents dancing together with me in their arms." What if the feelings are those of anxiety, dread, fear, even terror? What does it mean that many of the children work hard to avoid being in places where both parents might be expected to be present? What is the cost of "dreams" turning to "nightmares" as the writer of our opening e-mail remarks?

The cost for alienated parents being in the same place may be discomfort, embarrassment, hurt, pain, or even death. The television and newspaper regularly report stories similar to the following. This tragedy unfolds like fiction, but it is factual.

Rachel was graduated second in her class. She played in the band and was voted "most likely to succeed" by her classmates. She had aspirations of becoming a neurosurgeon. Rachel's dreams ended with a nightmare. Her abusive father, whom her mother had divorced a year prior, attended Rachel's high school graduation. He was reported saying, "Wouldn't nobody talk to him" (at the event). This enraged him. Days later, he proceeded to go to the home of his ex-wife, daughter, and son. His ex-wife, cowering in the closet, begged for the life of her children and her own while on the phone with 911. He shot them all. He killed Rachel, and later his ex-wife died of her wounds in the hospital. His son was seriously wounded, but will recover from the physical wounds in time *(The Tennessean,* June 26 and 30, 2004).

This is the terror of some children who dread having both parents in the same place when violence has been a part of their lives. What will a parent who is drinking, angry, and hurt do? There will be all kinds of people around, but will that make any difference?

Of course, few events that are shared by alienated parents end in physical death; however, during many events the tension is palpable. Some *celebrations* cause inward wounds that act like a chronic illness in the life of the child. Every spring may bring reminders of graduation ceremonies that the child skipped so there would be no event where the parents might come into contact with each other. The anniversaries remind the couple that there are no pictures from the courtroom where they were married, because they could never decide how to get their parents, their parents' ex-spouses, and their current partners down the church aisle without someone feeling slighted. When there's already an overwhelming amount of grief, the failure of parents to act in a civil manner can bring additional grief and impede the healing that being together brings to many people.

Weddings are particularly painful for children of the switching hour. Joyful beginnings have a way of bringing to mind painful endings. All the complexities of a two-world existence emerge.

"If Dad has agreed to pay for our wedding, then his new wife must sit up front with him, because he's walking me down the aisle. Mom's parents offered to pay for the wedding so Dad wouldn't have so much say. Granddad offered to walk me down the aisle. But I've always dreamed that my wedding day would be perfect.

"Mom cries every time we start making wedding plans. Her wedding had taken Granddad years to pay for. He was still paying for the wedding when she asked him to help her pay for a divorce. He didn't mind. I am seriously worried that Mom will not make it through my wedding with just a few sniffles. She may do anything when Dad walks me down the aisle.

"It would be easier if Abram, my fiancé, could understand. His family is so loving and stable. Sometimes I think he believes that I am exaggerating how difficult working with my family is. It's like a volcano. There's a hot molten layer of anger underneath my mom and dad's cooled layers of divorce lava that spews out with even the mention of the word 'marriage.'

"Does it matter that Abram and I are young professionals in our community who really want to make a good impression on our friends and colleagues? We've been together so long and now we want to start our family, so we are getting married. We want to celebrate after the wedding with all our friends at the country club. We've saved

money for the reception, so Dad won't ruin the fun
by listing all the things he's *not* going to pay for.
He must have forgotten the glorious party that
Granddad threw for them. The pictures are amaz-
ing. Flowers were everywhere. (No small feat in
December in the Northeast!) Enough candles to
light a small village and a champagne fountain. If
planning a wedding is this hard, I dread thinking
about how my parents will act at our kids' birthday parties, ball games, and concerts. Okay, one
thing at a time. But my stomach tightens at the
thought of it."

For children, the breakup or divorce of their parents is
never *over*. Your children live in the world between you.
When events in life call for you both to be in the same place,
remember that your child (whether he or she is three or
thirty) will be particularly sensitive to how you conduct
yourselves. They are forever testing the intensity of the tension between the two of you.

"The thing that bothers me the most is that my
mother wouldn't let my father and his new wife,
who was his companion of fifteen years, sit with us
at the funeral for my sister. My mother and father
had been divorced for fourteen years, but that did
not matter. Dad was not to sit with the rest of us.
She said, 'He wanted the divorce, so too bad for
him.'

"I'll tell you one thing; he didn't want my sister to die. He gave her the best care money could

buy. She shared my mom's addictive personality, so at eighteen, she had already been through four eating disorder clinics.

"When her boyfriend decided he liked someone else, he tried to let her down easily. But my sister got so depressed. She said, 'All men are just the same. They're all like Dad. Bro, if you turn out like Dad, I'll hate you.'

"After staying in her room for days, she came out one morning and said she felt better. Mom and I were glad for that. She hadn't even binged and purged like before. We didn't know where she went that afternoon, but later learned she had called her friends and told them she wanted to go out to eat so she could celebrate her new life. She now was a free woman. They ate, drank, and talked for hours. They hadn't seen her that happy in weeks. Sis only had a couple of drinks, so she seemed okay to drive. What they didn't know was that she had a bottle of Mom's wine in the car. After the party broke up, she drove to her favorite park, wrote us each a letter, and mailed them. Then she drove over the cliff of the mountainside she loved the most. At first we thought it was an accident, that she was drunk. Then the letters came. It wasn't because she was drinking.

"We didn't see it coming. We'd be smarter now. But it's too late. Why can't Mom let Dad sit with us? Please, God, help me not be like Dad or Mom."

I TRY TO AVOID REPEATING MY PARENTS' MISTAKES

Learning from the mistakes of others so we don't have to make the same mistakes ourselves is part of life's education. This bit of wisdom should help us, right? If you are a child of the switching hour, however, your parents' mistakes may paralyze you. You may have decided that you don't ever want to risk the possibility of repeating your parents' mistakes. You don't want to experience the heartaches you see in your parents such as being poor, fighting continually, or begging for child support. Maybe you don't ever want to have any child of yours move regularly between two worlds.

What does not wanting to repeat their parents' mistakes mean for children of the switching hour? It means that fewer children who have experienced their parents' alienation marry (Wallerstein, Lewis, and Blakeslee, 329). They are hesitant to make a lifetime commitment to another. Their capacity to trust another person has been shaken. What if this beloved person leaves them too?

> "I was engaged a couple of times, but I never got married. They were good women, but they wanted children. I couldn't do it. I couldn't ever risk a child feeling as sad and depressed as I've been since my fairytale life ended when my mother left. I've been commitment-phobic ever since."

As children of two worlds, they are less likely to have children of their own (Wallerstein, Lewis, and Blakeslee, 329). They know having a family does not necessarily mean that the two adults will face whatever challenges come their way together. Many are all too aware that illness, joblessness, military deployment, or housework doesn't always bring out the team spirit in parents. The children of the switching hour worry and are anxious about having a family.

> "What if my child also knows a divided life? Do you know how sick I always felt when they instructed us to draw our family tree in school? The teachers always asked about the bunches of people around my paper. 'That's *my family*,' I'd say. I dread trying to draw a family tree even today."

For some children, the divorce so disrupts their lives that they have a difficult time making plans and getting on track. They thought they knew who they were and where they were going, but now they are not sure. Drugs, alcohol, crime, or other "acting out" may be their attempts to deaden the pain or draw attention to their suffering.

> "I started drinking when the divorce happened. Dad said I was acting just like *her*. (Having someone tell you that you remind them of one of your parents is usually a good thing. However, when you're a child of the switching hour, it rarely is a compliment.) 'Why are you smoking pot, partying, and doing your art? Why aren't you taking accounting courses so you can assist me in the construction business? I've done all this for you.'
>
> "He has done it all for me—he's a regular workaholic. I didn't think I'd have to be doing anything but work for him. So, I quit college—

more time to drink and smoke pot. He doesn't seem to really need me one bit, despite what he says. My mother was always the bridge between the two of us. Not anymore! He's never here and Mom rarely calls. Life is not a challenge. Maybe I am just a bored coward? How's that for some philosophical reflections of a thirty-nine-year-old?

"My peace doesn't last when I visit my mother, either. For some reason, she still thinks I should be setting some goals for my life. 'You're not too old to be married! When am I going to have any grandchildren? And, what about that brilliant mind of yours?' Mom doesn't know that these words hurt me. She even offers to pay for me to finish college. I remind her that you need to care about the future to do that."

The Switching Hour

Yesterday, all my troubles seemed
        so far away,
Now it looks as though they're here
        to stay . . .
—John Lennon and Paul McCartney, "Yesterday"

CHAPTER SIX

THE HOUR I SPEND WITH GOD

Dear Grandpa,

I went to God's house today. But God's house here is nothing like God's house I visit when I'm with you. Your church has beautiful colored glass, dark wood, and is so quiet. The organ makes the music the angels hear, I'm sure. In Dad's church, we were there with about two thousand other people. They had a rock band and the place looked like a gym with a few plants at the front of it. God has many homes, Dad said. These two are as different as Mom and Dad's houses.

The people were nice, but I don't think they had a clue that this was my first visit with Dad. Do you think God will be mad at Mom for not going to church?

Guess what? The preacher talked about Jesus getting into trouble because he stayed at God's house when his family left town. Jesus must have two dads too, because he said that he was in his father's house, but Joseph and Mary were on their way home. So he was in one father's home, but he wasn't in his other father's house. Is that right? Maybe Jesus knows how I feel about my dad and stepdad.

Grandpa, I have some other questions for you. For years I prayed and prayed that Mom and Dad would quit fighting and get back together. I keep asking God to help Dad to stop being so angry all the time. It doesn't work.

Does God answer kids' prayers?

One more thing. Is God like my father? I think of Dad every time we pray, "Our Father, who art in heaven . . ." If God were like you, it would be great, but Dad? Sometimes he's fine, then again he's not. he looks like someone else when he's mad. The teacher said the Bible teaches I must honor—show respect—to my mom and dad. Dad always yells the same thing at me, but does she know my dad?

I hope you and Grandma are good. Are you watching your diet for your heart? I love you, you know. I still ask God to heal your heart.

Love,

H.

I'VE BEEN WONDERING

Step back into the days of your childhood for a moment. Do you remember being amazed by life's surprises? Where *did* your baby sister come from? How did the leaves appear on the trees each spring? What about those thunderstorms that seemed to shake your home apart with each boom?

Perhaps your wondering moved you into the realm of the Holy. You may have had questions about what God looks like or is like. "Where does God live?" you may have asked. And, "Does Jesus see me all the time just like Santa Claus does?"

You wondered in amazement and you were full of questions. Children of the switching hour wonder, too. Their wondering in amazement and awe may delight or irritate you, depending on your own spiritual interest. The questions will either push you as a parent to examine your own views of life's mysteries and the divine, or cause a reflex of anger and rejection that shuts down your child's questioning.

THE HOUR I SPEND WITH GOD

Wondering, asking questions, probing, and clarifying are how children learn and make sense of their lives. When there has been a major shift in their lives as they have known it, they will wonder and question even more. Many children believe that surely the Holy One (or however they name their sense of the divine) knows the answers to their questions.

Consider the wide diversity of religions around the globe. One could do doctoral work in world religions and still not be able to explain all the differences between and within religious groups. The spiritual self-understanding within any given group is distinct as well. Imagine being a *child* and trying to make sense out of dramatically different religious teachings and styles.

GOD HAS MORE THAN ONE HOUSE, TOO!

> "When I first had two houses to call home, I felt so alone. All my friends at that time had one room that was theirs, one home, and one address. One day I started to count houses that God was said to occupy in the small city where my mother and I live. There were seventy-five different houses: small ones and large ones—brick ones, wooden ones, cement ones, too—churches, synagogues, temples, mosques, holy sites, and gathering places. People find God in each of those places. I don't feel so alone, now. Wow! If I counted all the places around the world, I would need a computer to help me keep track of them all. Think of all those addresses. What about all the people? Does God really know each of us, just as God remembers the sparrows?" [See Luke 12:6-7.]

The sense of God's expansive presence is celebrated in the musings of this child. However, sometimes it is religious differences between the couple that cause or contribute to the breakup. As individuals mature, the significance of religious commitments may take on more meaning for one or both, and, on occasion, push the partners in opposite directions. It is a transition that not all couples are able to navigate.

Children are full of questions about the One whom they regard as holy and powerful. Listen as the children wonder about the holy and overhear what they say to religious leaders.

Does God miss me when I'm gone?

"My mom and dad fight about my going to church with Dad's parents all the time. My grandparents pick me up for Mass on Saturday every week. After Mass we go to our favorite restaurant. All their friends come up and ask me how I've been. Whether I'm at Mom's or Dad's, my grandparents still come and get me for Mass. Lately, Mom's started to get angry about this when she has me. She says she doesn't want me to be hurt by the priest. I don't know what she's talking about. Father Joe is wonderful to all of us. Granddad changes channels when anything about priests comes on TV. I just want to keep going to Mass with my grandparents. It's one of the few things that has stayed the same in my life since the divorce."

Adults know that religious discussions are full of energy and emotion. History and tradition are more powerful for some individuals than for others.

"This synagogue [this temple, this mosque, or this church] was the worship center for my great grandparents, my grandparents, parents, and our family until the divorce. I will not leave now."

That kind of continuity in one's life of faith is sustaining for some as they move through the divorce experience. For others, the religious home becomes a place of judgment and condemnation; they may feel God-forsaken as well.

Whether or not children are able to worship in the manner that has been their previous custom depends, for the most part, upon you—their parents and stepparents—and your willingness to transport them, or upon the generosity of other members who will stop by, if there is parental approval. Children look to the warmth of others in the religious community for encouragement during the challenging days of the switching hours. Often a youth leader, choir director, or an instructor is trained to notice those who are struggling and hurting.

"I wonder if God misses me when I'm gone. I've been with Mom and Greg for the summer. Mom is totally against the whole 'church thing' and gets angry if I ask about attending the church up the street. 'Where were they when we needed them?' she asks. I can't help it that the members quit talking to her after the divorce. Yes, they treated me like I was invisible when I used to attend afterwards, but I know God sees me. Ms. Smith, the Sunday school teacher, is always glad to see me, asks me how I've been, and tells me she's missed me. I really hoped that I could get a perfect attendance pin this year, but Mom and Greg think all that's nonsense. So, once again, I'm many Sundays short. Do you think God misses me when I'm gone?"

Rites of passage are important in our lives. Remember getting your driver's license, leaving home, or your first job? There are religious rites of passage as well. Being denied the opportunity to be baptized or to celebrate a First Communion or Confirmation is not readily forgotten. Being able to celebrate a bar or bat mitzvah if you are Jewish is central to many young people's identity. They want to be faithful. Being prevented from living out one's religious commitments because of parental opposition is difficult for children to understand.

"I really wanted to have my bar mitzvah this year so all my friends and I would always remember this most sacred time we each had experienced. Of course, the celebrations are great fun as well. However, it was not to be. I had parents who thought that being an interfaith couple was intriguing. They said that I'd have opportunity to explore a broader religious vision. All this was true until the divorce. I begged my Jewish father to reason with my Christian mother. Doesn't she remember that Jesus was Jewish? She hadn't cared that my father had made sure that I kept the Sabbath and went to Hebrew school. Now it mattered. Since the divorce, she delighted in removing from our lives anything that reminded her of my father. I had to hide all my religious treasures.

And, most sadly, she would not be persuaded that my bar mitzvah was important enough for her to set aside her anger with my father *for the sake of this important event in my life.* With each of my friend's bar mitzvah celebrations, I grew more depressed. I've stopped coming out of my room now unless she forces me to come out and eat."

God is like *my* father?

Children, like adults, ponder the nature of God. When in places of worship, they may hear that God is their "father." Those who are Christian learn that Jesus called God, *"Abba"* or "Daddy" when he prayed (Mark 14:36). This sets off musings such as those of the letter writer, *H.*, who opened this chapter. He wondered if God was like the one he called Daddy. Children are concrete thinkers. If you tell a young child that there is a man in the moon, they look for the man. Or if you tell them that God is their father, then all aspects of their fathers are projected onto God—positive and negative, including being absent if this is the case with their fathers.

"God is like *my* father? I wonder about that! When I pray 'Our Father in Heaven' I think of my dad who is in heaven. He was a Vietnam veteran who my mother said was so sweet and quiet when she married him. After the war, there wasn't any sweetness left, let me assure you of that. Any little thing would set off angry tirades. He would cuss for a half hour straight. We learned to be so careful in his presence so as to not set him off yet again. He and a friend died in a car wreck after too many beers in a local tavern. Now I know he had post-traumatic stress disorder that went untreated. I didn't know it then, nor did my mother. God in heaven, be good to my father who suffered here quite enough."

While sometimes the idea that God is like our parents may be troubling, at other times it is greatly comforting to those who seek a protector and a guardian.

"Daddy kept me safe when Mommy was mad. She spanked me real hard with her wooden spoon. He'd tell her to stop hurting his precious girl. I sure wish he still lived here so he could help me now. Mommy's mad all the time. She smells funny, too. She tells me it's the incense. My teacher sniffs me when I go to school. Is God like my Daddy?"

Having more than two people in your life who function as mother and father is a common experience for children of the switching hour. Whether their parents remarry or live with someone after a divorce, they are expected to give the adults respect and obedience. H., our letter writer, was delighted to learn that Jesus had two fathers. As he listened to the preacher discuss Jesus' remaining in the synagogue while Mary and Joseph (his earthly father) left so Jesus could be "in my Father's house," H. was comforted by the realization that Jesus had two homes and two fathers as well. Jesus lived in two worlds. He had a heavenly father and an earthly father.

There are times when a parent's behavior has damaged the title of father or mother in such a way that a person will never be able to receive any comfort from a divine being when praying "Father" or "Mother."

"I can't pray the 'Our Father'," she said. "I just can't do it." She stopped, silent, wide-eyed, and sad. I waited. Slowly the words came. "He sexually abused me," she stammered. "My father abused me." More silence. "Who is good and loving to you? Who protects you? Comforts you when you are sad?" I asked. "My grandmother," came her swift and solid reply. "Then God is like your grandmother," I said gently. "Can you imagine God being like your grandmother?" She nodded slowly, smiled, opened the door, and left.

QUESTIONS FOR YOU, GOD

Children of the switching hour are full of questions: Did I cause the divorce by fighting all the time? If I kept my room cleaner would that have helped? Would my father or mother have stayed if I didn't have so many medical problems? Will my parents ever get back together again? Will I be able to stay married? They have questions for God as well: What about my unanswered prayers? What does it mean that a father should not cause his child to be angry? Are you with me now? Do you travel, God?

What about my unanswered prayers?

"I prayed and prayed that what Mommy and Daddy told me wasn't true. I don't want to leave Daddy. I know my twin sister doesn't either. My teacher said Minnesota is a long long way from California. I can't even spell Minnesota by myself. She said it snows there. We don't have cold weather clothes. I like the beach. Do lakes have waves? I don't want to leave Daddy. God, why aren't you changing Mommy and Daddy's minds? Pastor says you hear us when we pray. Why aren't you answering me? You do miracles, the Bible says. Will you do a miracle for me?"

What does it mean that I should "Honor my father and mother"?

"I get upset every time I hear my mom and dad tell me that I should 'honor' them (Exodus 20:12; Matthew 19:19). It's so hard to honor parents when they are so obsessed with paying the right amount of money for child support or who has the most new possessions. When I question them about money for straightening my bad teeth or saving for college I get slapped down and told that I better respect them so things will go well for me in my life. God, does this mean I have to be quiet? When I am with Mom she runs down Dad. At Dad's, I hear things about Mom I don't even want to know.

"The other Sunday, the minister preached about fathers not causing their children to be angry or the children 'may lose heart' (Colossians 3:21). I nearly fell off the pew. Maybe I was dreaming, I thought. But my sister said she read the same thing in the Bible during her meditation time. How do we get along, God, when everyone is so stressed and mad? What does honoring my father and mother look like? Should they honor me, too?"

God, are you with me now?

"I know you have many houses after I started to look around. But God, I'm wondering if you travel. Do you know what it's like to spend hours of your life listening to the hum of tires on the road or to feel the pull on your body as the airplane takes off for one more departure? Do you know what constant arrivals and departures feel like?

"I asked my religion teacher this question. She pointed me to stories of the Exodus. The Hebrew people left slavery and Egypt (Exodus 13:17–14:31). God had heard their cries and led them out. You'd think they would have been glad to be out of there, but they missed the good things about the bad old days. I can relate to that. While they were traveling and complaining in the middle of their new freedom, God promised to be with them. God was a pillar of cloud by day and a pillar of fire by night (Exodus 13:21-22). God travels.

"I've worried that you'll leave me, God, if I'm bad. Dad said he couldn't stand my constant trouble at school. He got sick of my running away and stealing when I was a kid. He'd had enough. But I read some more about the Hebrew people. They kept getting in trouble and you kept seeking them out. I know you'll come find me if I wander off. Something about lost sheep comes to mind (Luke 15:3-7).

"For Christians, she said Jesus offers reassurance when he leaves them. According to the gospel of Matthew, Jesus said, 'And remember, I am with you always, to the end of the age' (Matthew 28:20). I am not alone in my switching, waiting, hoping, wishing, avoiding, and wondering. God, you travel with me."

I WONDER IF RABBIS, PRIESTS, IMAMS, PASTORS, MINISTERS, RELIGIOUS LEADERS OF EVERY TYPE AND THEIR CONGREGATIONS THINK ABOUT US—THE SWITCHING HOUR CHILDREN?

Children are sensitive to language and actions that include or exclude them. They wonder if they are valued members of a faith community. Do you ostracize children for the decisions their parents make? If a child doesn't do their memory work or show up for religious school on time, or at all, remember these are not always his or her choices.

During times of intense change and transition, the things we consider to be routine and ordinary fall by the wayside. Parents sometimes feel they are doing great just to get their children clothed and fed. Many women, and some men, now work two jobs to sustain the life of their family after a separation or divorce. How much do you know about the everyday lives of those who look to you for compassion and care? Have you thought about what your religious community can do to help us, the children and families with switching hour lives?

CHILDREN OF THE SWITCHING HOUR ASK, "PLEASE WATCH YOUR LANGUAGE"

"We live a unique existence. We have two 'homes,' two locations in which we strive to feel comfortable and at peace. Our parents are separate even if they are united in their love and care for us. We rarely—maybe never—have the comfort of a group hug with both parents. We have lost so much and accommodated even more. We have adjusted. But, I'm wondering, do you think about us? Do you remember that not all children live with both parents? There are stepparents we love, or adults who share our household not bound to us with anything but love, or perhaps necessity. Some of my friends don't have a father. They don't expect to ever know him.

"Please don't whisper about me when I worship with my father and his new girlfriend. I'm really shy. Being talked about and avoided only makes my family and me want to stay away. I'm still the same person. Oh yeah, I hurt more, am distracted and in a daze, but maybe this will pass. I could really use some kindness. Isn't that what being 'religious' is all about?

"On Mother's Day and Father's Day, remember that not all of our parents are of the Hallmark variety. Please watch your language in prayers and in preaching. The day brings longing and pain, especially if this wasn't our weekend to be with the parent being celebrated. If we have been abandoned by this adult in our lives, the pain is even greater. Do we honor stepfathers and stepmothers who love us as their own? If they choose not to love us, the rejection of us by someone our parent loves is excruciating. We are not all happy families."

HIGH DAYS OF CELEBRATION BRING ME LOW

Events of great significance are especially difficult for children of the switching hour. No loved one is to be left out, but how will they get along in the same space for any length of time? Where's the joy of a Confirmation service when parents glare at each other when they and their new spouses came to the front of the church to be part of blessing their child during the service?

"I used to love the holidays until my parents divorced. Now we aren't together in joyous reunion ever. Preachers of all types, please remember that I'm thinking about my loved ones I'm not with, even as I'm smiling, praying, and singing with you here."

DAYS OF MOURNING BRING ME LOWER

"Will Dad's first wife (not my mother) be here for my sister? Will my mother, Dad's third wife, be present for me? Our brother's unexpected death (born during Dad's second marriage) has sent us all reeling. He couldn't wait until he got his driver's license, but winter is a bad time to start driving. The semi-truck driver couldn't see him as Brian struggled to get his new car into the right gear. He just had to have a stick shift! Here we are—together and separate—at the same time. I don't even want to think of what it will be like when Dad dies. Will you think of us in the midst of this family web when you care for us?"

PLEASE MAKE US FEEL AT HOME

"Do you know how hard an every-other-weekend life is? I can't possibly keep Kosher, because my mother thinks my Dad's a fanatic. Rabbi, do you understand my struggle? It helps me when you remember that I am away not because of my own choice. Please help me think of ways to feel connected even though I'm only half-time. Everyone is so kind and loving here. They know my name. I feel my true self in this congregation."

ARE THERE SCRIPTURE PASSAGES AND PRAYERS TO HELP WITH MY SWITCHING HOUR YEARS?

"My friend has been really sick since she was little. Mary goes to St. Jude Children's Research Hospital for her cancer. She is in and out of the hospital. Her priest helped her make a book of readings and prayers. Do you think you could help me make something to take with me for my years of switching, waiting, hoping, wishing, avoiding, and wondering?"

Ask your religious leader for prayers and readings from the sacred texts to help your children as they live the switching hour years.

The Switching Hour

The LORD will keep
   your going out and your coming in
   from this time on and forevermore.
   —Psalm 121:8

THE SWITCHING HOUR REVISITED

Dear Mom,
(I'm giving a copy of this letter to Papa, too.)

The years of my childhood Switching Hours are over —
all twelve of them. This fall I'll head to college
in Boston, too far from either of you to make one
of you feel jealous that I have picked a favorite.

For the last time I have left my beloved dog Elijah
in order to come to be with you, my beloved mother,
for the summer in San Francisco. You and Lynn
are great. I love the city and your smart friends.
The university is such a rich and marvelous
place to meet people from around the world.

Speaking of worlds — sometimes I feel like I've
lived twelve years on two separate planets. Your
life is so different from the one I live with Papa.
The rolling green hills, horses, and barns of
Kentucky are beautiful. The country house is huge
and so quiet with only Papa and me.

I don't think many of my school friends
understand our trips to Europe for Christmas and
the Bahamas for Easter that you, Lynn, the kids,
and I take. They think I dress weirdly when
I come back, too. I've never been able to
describe my split — two-world — life to them.
Superman would get it.

Forgive me Mom (and Papa), but I pray that
my kids (if I ever have any) will never have
twelve years of constantly shuttling between
two worlds, always lonely for the parent and
the place where he or she is not.

I promise to visit you both, but please don't
keep track of the days, hours, and minutes.
You aren't in charge of my life forever.
I'll do my best to be fair.

Love, P.

LIFE HAS CHANGED FOREVER

Remember the day that you became a parent? The date is probably clearly etched in your memory. Life as you knew it was changed forever by the birth of your child. You were now a father or a mother. Nothing will alter that reality—you *are* a parent.

Life is now lived through your eyes and the eyes of your children. Becoming a parent changes life in ways both large and small—everything from living space to vehicles that have car seats, sleeping and eating patterns, and how you spend your money and time. Life is different!

In a way similar to your becoming a parent, the life of a child is changed by your decision to divorce or separate. Life is changed forever. Everyday, ordinary things are different. They are now children whose parents do not live in one place, but two. As people who care for our children, it is our job to make that life as happy and as stress free as possible.

PARENTS AND CHILDREN OF THE SWITCHING HOUR HAVE DIFFERENT POINTS OF VIEW

It may be hard for you to do all that your children need or ask you to do, but think about this:

1. Your children love both of you.

They want and need both of you to love them and to be dedicated to taking care of them. No matter how awful you think the other parent is, no matter how terrible they were to your children, a child does not give up caring for a parent and wishing they'd be different. The children will deny that the separation is real and will try everything from being sick, to getting in trouble, to being extra good to get you back together.

2. Your child needs more from you when you have less energy and love to give.

A child needs more love, hugs, and reassurance when you are full of grief and are sad, confused, or angry. You may be exhausted from doing all that is required to start over. At the time you are more focused on your own pain and suffering, the children need you to pay added attention to them. They may be so concerned about your happiness that they will hide their own unhappiness and misery. Whether they are able to tell you or not, assume they need more care and comfort. Spend time with each of your children. It may be as simple as eating a meal together at the table or reading a bedtime story to them. A hug or squeeze around the shoulder lets them know you love them.

3. You and your children may want opposite things. While you're trying to have a life without the other parent and any reminders of him or her, your children are trying to keep things the same.

You want distance from the other parent, they want closeness. You want infrequent contact; they want as much or more contact with both parents. You would like to toss pictures and any items that are from that person. The pictures and gifts comfort and remind the children of the parent that they are away from and miss. The absence of the parent is a huge change for them. Even when the other parent was often away, the children expected that the parent would still return.

4. Because you are an adult, you've already learned how to go through changes in your life; whether that means leaving home after school, having your body grow, or having your feelings of love change.

Children can't adjust to change as easily or quickly as an adult can. It's like asking a child to drive a car before they've ridden a tricycle. Your child will need time to grow up before some of the changes you've already made are possible for them. Their minds and bodies are still developing. They may not have the understanding or language skills to respond to all the new and different aspects of their lives.

DIVORCE IS A VERB

Even though you remember the day that you became a parent, you have many other significant memories of parenthood. Being a parent means parenting. It's an ongoing, lifelong process that takes continual learning and practice.

For children whose parents divorce or separate, their experience of the divorce or separation is similar. Parents move on from the divorce or separation day and create a new home with additional duties, often finding another partner. There is a sense of a "new normal" after a period of time. The children, however, move between the parents for as long as the separated parents are living and are in relationship with their children. They live the verb divorce: bags packed for traveling.

Divorce as a verb means taking legal action to end a marriage. For the children the action of divorce is not securing an official piece

*of paper or the day one of the parents says, "I'm leaving for good."
It is all the switching hours that are* necessary *for staying in touch
with both parents who no longer live in the same place.*

The action of divorce ranks high on charts rating stressful
life events for adults and their children. Even events that we
consider necessary or good are stressful and require time for
adjustment. How can you help children with this new life?
You can begin by listening with your heart to your children
and, for a little while, putting yourself in their place. By
finding the strength to do this, you will be caring for your
children and giving them the love they need.

THE SWITCHING HOURS REVISITED

You are helping your children by reading this book and
thinking about what life is like walking in their shoes. *The
Switching Hour: Kids of Divorce Say Good-bye Again* highlights
some of what your child or children may be experiencing and
suggests several ways you may reduce the stress of the
switching hour.

Chapter 1: The Switching Hour explored the losses and
consequences of life lived between parents. *Switching* is the
word that carries the experiences of loss, change, and constant
transition or traveling between parents. This chapter noted the
sadness, grief, guilt, and losses that are part of the stress of the
lives of children who travel between parents as a way of life.

Chapter 2: The Hour I Wait and Long For described
the *waiting* that the children do in their lives that are
divided between homes. While they are *at home* in one place,
they are *away from another home*. They must adjust to the

leaving, waiting, and coming back every time they move to the other parent's home. This chapter highlighted the feelings of a child who is always lonely for the other parent and the place where he or she is not.

Chapter 3: The Hour I Hope Comes, But Does Not reminded us that children are people of hope. *Hoping* describes the hearts of children who long for things to be different, for their deep desires to come true, for painful realities to change.

This chapter addressed two core issues in the lives of many children whose parents are no longer together: absent parents and parents who have not recovered from the divorce. Fathers and mothers *both* are important to the healthy development of sons and daughters alike. Children yearn for an absent parent.

If you are a parent who has not recovered from separating from your child's other parent, it is time to find some help. Parents Without Partners is an organization of people who will understand you and your busy life. This is not a time to just "buck up" and go it alone. You will help your child by finding a divorce recovery group, counselor, or religious leader to help you through this transition in your life, so you are able to care for your children. Children are overwhelmed with taking care of parents who cry all the time, who go to their room and sleep, who bring many different dates home, or who are drinking or stoned.

Chapter 4: The Hour I Wish Wouldn't Come described the *wishing* of children as they dread upcoming events that they find hard or sad. This chapter discussed the interruptions that come into the lives of children who live divided lives, and how they wish the fun didn't have to end because of the hour of the day or the day of the week. Children's desires for Mommy's and Daddy's new house to stay the same were explored. Two other core issues for the children were also addressed: troubled parents and shared holidays.

Parents, when you hear reports from your child or others that there is one, or several, significant mental health issues with the other parent—suspected physical or sexual abuse, addiction, depression, or violence—it is time to evaluate the situation for your child's safety. If you see bruises, blood in their underwear, if they have trouble sitting down, have urinary tract infections, tell you that monsters visit them in their beds at night, act out in a hypersexual manner, or are terrified about leaving you, **you must act**. This will involve discussing your concerns and the reports of the child or children with professionals. Speak with a psychologist, pastoral counselor, or child psychiatrist. Call a domestic violence or rape and sexual abuse center for advice about what to do for your child. They will help direct you. If your child is in immediate danger, always call 911.

Holidays may just be another day for you, but children (with the help of TV and the movies) build up grand visions. Your child will feel especially loved if you take the time to plan ahead and are able to tell them what they will be doing for the special days in your home and when they will be with the other parent. Kids value having happy parents and suffer when a parent is alone on a holiday.

Chapter 5: The Hour I Try to Avoid described the *avoiding* activity of children of the switching hour who seek not to experience previously painful events *again*. This hour focuses on the significant life events that are avoided as well as life choices such as marriage and children, which are contemplated with great ambivalence.

Here is another place (in addition to your own improved health and well-being) where all the personal work of healing that you have been able to do as parents pays off. When you are able to be in the other parent's presence for the sake of your children—even though you may intensely dislike the other parent (and assuming, of course, they are not given to violence or extreme mental illness)—you will enable your children to be free of some of the divided life of the switching hour.

Chapter 6: The Hour I Spend With God holds the *wondering* that is directed to the Holy One by children of the switching hour. Children's sense of awe and the comfort of familiar rituals, as well as the possibility of other adults showing an interest in them, draw children to religious communities. This chapter focused on how children equate parenting imagery of God with their own parents and highlighted the significance of the religious community's influence on children. It also drew our attention to the support children need to grow spiritually, given that they often travel when religious services take place and may be away a significant amount of time.

Chapter 7 (this chapter): **The Switching Hour Revisited** and the chapter that follows, **How Can I Help?** provide an opportunity to review and suggest more ways to make the lives of the children more bearable.

THE CLOCK SAYS IT'S TIME FOR THE SWITCHING HOUR

What can reduce a child's stress during the ongoing years of switching hours? What will increase his or her sense of security, trust, ability to attach and love, as well as enhance the child's self-esteem? The following suggestions are offered as a beginning point. Your children will have requests of their own to add. Talk to them about it.

1. Make a Parenting Plan and adjust it as your children grow or as life's events dictate.

A Parenting Plan is what the words suggest: it is a plan that helps you decide *how* you both will parent your children. The Parenting Plan has at its heart the best interests of your children. It covers the specific details of when the children will be with each parent (including holidays, birthdays, etc.), insurance, financial support, education, and religious upbringing. It has great potential for reducing the daily conflict that may be involved in the switching hour life for you and your children. Tennessee, Alaska, Arizona, and other states have good Parenting Plan models.

- The Parenting Plan model for Alaska is found at: http://www.state.ak.us/courts/parenting.htm
- The model for Arizona is located at: http://www.supreme.state.az.us/dr/Text/ModelPTPlans.htm
- In Tennessee search: http://www.tsc.state.tn.us/geninfo/programs/Parenting/Parenting.htm

If at all possible, keep lines of communication open to discuss health issues and be together on the discipline of children, especially in the teenage years. Include stepparents in the discussion. A unified, loving front is best for children.

2. Please keep the agreed-upon switching hours.

Be a dependable parent, doing what you have promised. Sometimes you will need to go the extra mile for the sake of your children. As your children grow older, it may require changing the time and frequency of transitions. Be open to hearing from them and responding.

Share the burden of driving with the other parent. Be on time; call if you're not. Keep your cell phone charged. Your children will have greater trust and confidence in you. If you will not be the one to pick up the children, let the other parent and the child know. Having your new significant other pick up a child as a surprise may create anxiety or conflict. Greet your children as soon as you see them. Ask them how they are.

3. Resist the urge to make your child into a messenger or a mediator between you and the other parent.

The impulse to be mad at the messenger is great. Adults may understand each other. Children should not have to figure out all the possible meanings of a parent's actions or words. Don't involve them in conflicts with the other parent or vent about fights with the other parent. Speak to the other parent directly, or find a professional mediator through local bar or mediation associations to help you talk to the other parent.

4. Don't use the switching time or the drive to your home as an opportunity to grill your children about what is happening in the other parent's life or to put the other parent down.

Children do not appreciate being prodded about the other parent's new love interests, or how they spend their money, handle discipline, or if they keep their home clean. It is important that you simply receive what your children share with you and only ask further questions when you are concerned about their safety.

5. Make sure that your children have a bedroom and a place to store their belongings in the homes of both parents.

No one likes to feel as though they are in the way or have no privacy, especially teenagers. Ask your children what they need to feel at home with each of you.

When it is time for your child to leave your home, help them gather their belongings so that they do not have the stress of needing a book, DVD player, or a piece of sports equipment because they have left without it.

6. Do your part of the parenting when the children are with you.

The switching hour life means that the child's dirty laundry must be cleaned in two homes. Mealtime and bedtime in the two homes may be quite different, causing your child to be overtired or cranky because they are hungry. Take them to school, sports, music lessons, or appointments with the doctor and dentist if you live in the same town. Being a good parent, you will want to pay attention to these things. In addition, the learning of skills and the doing of homework must be accomplished in both settings. The switching, which the clock regulates, goes much more smoothly when the child returns fed and well rested, with clean clothes in the bag, and the homework completed.

7. Don't make your child choose a favorite between the two of you. Allow them to have affection for stepparents, too.

Your desire to be the *chosen* parent may be strong, especially if you feel rejected. But if you *win* this one, your child loses. Children need to feel love for and from both parents. Creating the feeling in your child that they are disloyal to you if they love or miss the other parent is a pressure that brings misery to a child's life. They are *Mommy's **and** Daddy's* children. Buying the love of your child is no substitute for your dedicated and loving parenting.

8. Use the switching hour as a time to show your children how much you care for them. Listen to your children and they will learn to listen, too.

How are your sons and daughters doing? It is important that you *listen* to them and watch their body language to learn what is going on for your sons and daughters. Even though you may feel the urge to talk about the divorce or separation with your children, constant questioning will not make them open up to you. Your most important task will be to listen to their concerns and worries, reassuring them when you can and letting them express all their feelings when they need to release stress or anger as well as sadness and grief.

You will need to be patient, asking open-ended questions rather than ones that they can answer with a yes or no. If you ask them if they had a good time while they were with their other parent, a "yes" or "no" may be all you hear. If you say, "Tell me what you did that you liked most while you were with your Mom," the child will be invited to share about something they enjoyed.

The switching hour life may go on for years. It is important that you periodically *ask your children*, "What would make your experience of living in two homes and traveling between them easier?" Be prepared to work with them in doing what you can to change that which is hard or painful for them.

Some children will be too young, or older children may be unable to find the words, to tell you what they feel or want. You will need to learn the body language of each of your children. Body language is how your child looks, or doesn't look at you, in a manner that is respectful according to your culture. It is how children will or will not let you embrace or kiss them if that is your custom. Are they energized and busy, or do they sleep way more than is usual for them? How is your child's appetite? Has he or she stopped eating? Are your children cleaning out the refrigerator? Have you noticed cuts or deep scrapes on their arms or legs? They may hide this by wearing long sleeves and long skirts or pants *all* the time. Do they smile (at least occasionally) and look relaxed or are they tearful and withdrawn? Are they angry all the time? How do the children treat each other?

Your children will give you clues as to how they are doing, even if they are too little to talk, if you take the time to look for them. Each child is different, to be sure; how your daughter and son let you know what they're feeling may be totally opposite. It is important for you to know how each of your children responds to pain and stress. Often this will change as they get older.

THERE ARE CLUES THAT TELL YOU THAT EVERYTHING IS NOT OKAY WITH YOUR CHILD.

Children too young to talk will show they are upset by doing things that you thought they had outgrown. They may suck on their fingers or thumb, wet the bed, and not put down their favorite comfort toy or blanket. You may also notice that they are stuck to you like Super Glue and will holler and cry if you leave the room. They fear that since one parent has left them, you may too.

Slightly older children will express their grief and sadness with many tears and periods of longing. They may ask when you are getting back together or what they did to make Dad or Mom leave.

As children grow older and are able to understand someone else's feelings, they may *choose sides* in response to answers that have been given or withheld from them. Sometimes it is an attempt to heal the hurt of missing a loved parent who is absent. A child may think that if they *don't care* about the absent parent they won't hurt as much. One hopes that the anger and hurt will be expressed and not silently bottled up in the child's effort to *be good* and not cause his or her parents pain or upset.

As life unfolds, teenagers are naturally moving away from their parents and toward friends and activities outside the home. They may let you know they're suffering through use of drugs and alcohol, promiscuous sex, a significant change in their academic or sports performance, or trouble with the law.

Even a *perfect* child may suffer silently in anguish and need to talk about feelings. Talking about feelings with a warm, listening person really can help. A deep fear for *any* person is feeling forgotten and alone. Talking has a way of reducing fear and building trust. It is important to note that even if your son or daughter is meeting all the expected markers of childhood and of the teenage years, this does not mean that they don't have feelings that are hard for them to share with you, but might do so if given the opportunity.

If your children aren't able to speak with you for fear of hurting you, they may be greatly helped by attending groups offered by schools or religious communities for children who share their experience. If your child's body language is troubling, if personality changes, if grades drop, or notes and conversations indicate severe pain or threats to end her or his life, it is time to ask a professional to help you.

TAKE CARE OF YOURSELF—IT'S A SWITCHING HOUR LIFE FOR YOU, TOO!

Children also benefit from knowing that you are okay. It is important for you to have support in being a parent (and person) who is no longer living with your child's other parent. There's no break in parenting duties for those who are upset about the end of a relationship. Even if you initiated the breakup, the sheer number of thoughts, feelings, and household changes that are involved in ending a relationship require you to invest a tremendous amount of extra energy elsewhere.

Now is not the time to pull back from your friends. Share meals as families. Form a cooperative for child care services. Exercise, do something for fun, find a group of people with whom to spend time, either around your spiritual life or pursuing a topic of interest. The children won't be wondering or worrying that all you do is lie on the couch when they are away from you. They will be encouraged knowing that you are learning and growing with them!

WHY ALL THIS FUSS? KIDS ARE STRONG!

The Switching Hour: Kids of Divorce Say Good-bye Again does not dismiss the idea that many children are able to *bounce back* and are *resilient*; however, this book draws attention to the stress of regular transitions and the energy required on the part of children to accomplish living in two homes and traveling between them, even when they appear to be doing just fine. It also intends to alert parents to the possibility that their child is not coping and needs extra attention.

A SWITCHING HOUR BLESSING

As a loving parent, do all that you can to make this time in your child's life happier and more peaceful. Children who are stressed need extra reassurance of your love and ongoing care for them.

A pastor asked, "What about a *Switching Hour* blessing of children by their parents?" Your message or blessing should let your children know the following: **I love you.** (The divorce or separation didn't change that.) **I will think of you while you are gone.** (I won't say "miss you" because I don't want you to feel guilty about leaving.) **Have fun.** (Yes, I know that your love for your Dad or Mom is good for you and me. Hate shrinks life. Your love will be enough for me, too.)

So when they leave, look your children in the eyes and say:
> **I love you.**
> **I will think of you when you are gone.**
> **Have fun.**

When they return, look them in the eyes and say:
   I love you.
   I thought about you while you were gone.
   I hope you had good days
      with your Dad/Mom.

Now, here is a blessing for you:
   Your children love you.
   They think of you when they are
      away from you.
   May all your days be filled with parenting joy
      as you love one another.

The Switching Hour

You're searching . . .
For things that don't exist;
   I mean beginnings.
Ends and beginnings—
   there are no such things.
There are only middles.
—Robert Frost, "In the Home Stretch"

CHAPTER EIGHT

HOW CAN I HELP?

"Daddy, say hello to Mommy."
Silence.
"Daddy! Say hello to Mommy."

More silence. Her daddy had just come into his former wife's house to pick up the children so that he could spend time with them. I overheard this plea thirty-five years ago; it has never left me:

"Daddy, say hello to Mommy."

How was this five-year-old to understand the silence? Sophia's parents were divorced now, but they were still her Mommy and Daddy, and she wanted them to be nice to one another.

Well, what had the ex-wife said or done that angered him? Or was it just the situation? Being divorced does not make a person a bad parent; however, it does make life *more*—more *challenging*, more *work*, and more *stressful*. Life is more *complex*. In the midst of the intensity, it is easy to be understanding about the tension between parents, but to ignore life as the child is experiencing it.

THE CHILD'S POINT OF VIEW

I was working with a colleague who was significantly taller than I. One day when I was standing on a stool, I realized that this was how he saw things all the time. The plates on the table seemed smaller. I saw the dust on top of the refrigerator, which hadn't bothered me until I was tall. I saw the top of my friend's head instead of his eyes when I talked to him. This was Tim's perspective! Now remember being small as a child. What might divorce feel like from the children's point of view? How is life for them?

Try to see life from the child's point of view as you consider these suggestions to make life simpler and to ease the transition for yourself and your children. Make notes here or in a notebook or journal.

1. THE SWITCHING HOUR

SWITCHING is the word that captures the experiences of loss, change, and constant transition that define the stress in the lives of the children of the switching hour, whose parents now live in separate locations.

In order to see life from my child's point of view, I will:
A. List all the changes my children have experienced because I no longer live with their other parent:

B. Think about and write down the losses my children have experienced. Why are they sad? What are they mourning? What are they grieving? (For example, they may be sad that the family is no longer one.):

C. Think of five things that I can do to keep some things the same in my child's life. (For example, you might decide that it is important to keep your children in the same school.):

D. Make sure that I know at least four things that will comfort my child or children when they are upset. (If you have more than one child, make a list for each of them. If you do not know, ask your children, if they are able to talk, or consult the other parent.):

E. Commit to having the things that comfort them available. (For example, if being rocked soothes a child, consider buying or borrowing a rocking chair. If they like to have books read to them, visit the library for books you may read to them or for books on tape. When they are babies and toddlers, you will need to make sure that you always gather the special toy or blanket to travel with them:

For further reading about loss, grief, and transitions, I suggest:
- Bridges, William B. *Transitions: Making Sense of Life's Changes, Revised 25th Anniversary Edition.* Cambridge, Mass.: Da Capo Press, 2004.
- Emery, Robert E. *The Truth about Children and Divorce: Dealing with the Emotions So You and Your Children Can Thrive.* New York: Plume, 2004.
- Trozzi, Maria. *Talking with Children about Loss: Words, Strategies, and Wisdom to Help Children Cope with Death, Divorce, and Other Difficult Times.* New York: The Berkley Publishing Group, 1999.

2. THE HOUR I WAIT AND LONG FOR

WAITING describes much of what children of the switching hour do in their lives. Theirs is a world filled with waiting and eager anticipation.

In order to see life from my child's point of view, I will:
A. Pay attention to my feelings when I wait. What goes through my mind?

B. Create a *Waiting Bag.* What will keep my child occupied if the other parent's arrival is delayed and I am not at home? (These activities might be travel games or flash cards that help your child with math or spelling. Be well supplied with necessities—a baby that is hungry or in dirty diapers is not happy.):

- Write a list of what you will put in your waiting bag. Is this something that you could give your child to help them wait for you? Do you need to make a waiting bag for yourself?

C. Pay attention to what helps me when I am missing my child. List the things that I can do to stay connected with my child or children. (Keep in mind that children need different things at different ages. Do you have recent pictures of your children placed where you see them each day? Are you faithful about phoning your children regularly when they are at the other parent's? If you don't like it when your child phones the other parent during *your time*, think about how happy you are to hear the voice of someone you care about who phones to see how you're doing.):

D. List four things that I can do to help my children stay connected with me when they are away from me. (For example, do you have a current picture that they may have to take with them? Do you make sure they are available when the other parent calls at the set time?):

- Since I know that my children miss the other parent, what can I do to help them stay connected with my ex?

For further reading I suggest:
- Baris, Mitchell A., and Carla B. Garrity. *Children of Divorce: A Developmental Approach to Residence and Visitation.* DeKalb, Ill.: Psytec Corporation, 1988.
- Families First, *TransParenting.* http://www.familiesfirst.org, or http://www.transparenting.com.

3. THE HOUR I HOPE COMES, BUT DOES NOT

HOPING describes the activity of children who long for things to be different with their parents, for their deep desires to come true, for painful realities to change.

Because I am willing to see life from my child's point of view, I will:

A. Be part of The Heartache Prevention Team! More important and impressive than any sports team—men's or women's—the THPT is for all those parents who are dedicated to being a central part of their child's life no matter what it takes. Make this a promise you will dedicate your life to keeping: I will not abandon my child, no matter how difficult things are for me. I will think first about my children.

- Write a statement affirming that you intend to be in your child's life for your whole life:

- Next, list the things you will have to do to make that happen:

B. Take steps to take care of myself. Am I eating, sleeping, and exercising? Am I going to work regularly? (If drugs or alcohol are a problem, join NA or AA. Are you still struggling because of the breakup or divorce? Are you angry, depressed, or numb and shut down? Find a divorce recovery group in your community and join it. Your religious leader may also suggest counselors who will work on sliding fee scales if money is tight and you want to do individual counseling.)

- These are areas that I am concerned about. (Make up your own symbols or notes if you don't want someone else to read this.):

C. Keep my financial commitments. I will pay the child support that is my responsibility. (List the concerns you have about doing this if you have any.) What do I need to do to make regular payments possible and on time?

D. Be fair to my children. Just because they remind me of the parent that I have left, I will not make remarks or put them down. (In what ways does your child remind you of his or her other parent? Make an effort to bring this to mind, so when you start to feel irritated you will remember this connection and will not take it out on your children.):

E. Be able to describe each of my children. How well do I really know them? (When was the last time you did something fun with your children? Buying things for them does not mean that you had fun.):

• I will do the following activities with my children:

For further reading, I suggest:
• Ellison, Sheila. *The Courage to Be a Single Mother: Becoming Whole Again after Divorce.* New York: HarperSanFrancisco, 2000.
• Knox, David. *Divorced Dad's Survival Book: How to Stay Connected with Your Kids.* Reading, Mass.: Perseus Books, 2000.

4. THE HOUR I WISH WOULDN'T COME

WISHING describes the inner world of children as they ponder and dread the hours they know must come.

Because I am willing to see life from my child's point of view, I will:

A. Pay attention to how I feel when something I enjoy will soon be coming to an end. What do I feel when a good time comes to a close? What is it like for me to miss someone dear? List what goes on inside of me when my child leaves and goes to the other parent's home. (Take time to notice yourself the next time if you are unable to answer it now.):

B. Be aware that leaving, switching, and re-entry for my children takes energy and may be difficult.

- To make life less stressful, I will take the following steps to make *leaving* easier. (For example, I will help gather my child's things before it is time to leave.):

- I will do these things to make the switching hour less difficult. (For example, I will leave on time.):

- So *re-entry* is more peaceful, I will do these things. (For example, I will give my children time to go to their rooms and I'll wait to talk with them until they're ready.):

C. Talk with my children before I make major changes in my life such as getting remarried or commit to moving out of state. I will make notes about the topics I will discuss with my children before I go ahead with my plans. I will share this with them when it seems right to do so. (This isn't "asking permission"; you are discussing important changes that will affect their lives in significant ways.):

D. Take seriously the reports from my children about the other parent's substance abuse, violence, and sexual and physical abuse. (As the writer of chapter four's opening letter and the story of the child who reports someone touched her private parts in the night relate, the addiction, abuse, and violence are real. The law states that suspected abuse of children, including your own, must be reported to the authorities for them to investigate.):

E. Take time to plan birthdays, holidays, and vacations with the other parent well in advance so work schedules, travel arrangements, and the children's school and activity schedules may be coordinated. What is the next event that I should be planning?

For further reading, I suggest:
- Ricci, Isolina. *Mom's House, Dad's House: Making Two Homes for Your Child.* New York: Simon & Schuster, 1997.
- Schneider, Meg F., and Joan Zuckerberg. *Difficult Questions Kids Ask—and Are Too Afraid to Ask—About Divorce.* New York: Fireside, 1996.

5. THE HOUR I TRY TO AVOID

AVOIDING is the chief activity of children of the switching hour who seek to not experience previously painful events yet again. They maneuver and scheme, walk on eggshells, and try extra hard to avoid the suffering.

Because I am willing to see life from my child's point of view, I will:

A. Consider what upsets me most about being around my child's other parent. (Recall the writer of the opening letter who eloped so her parents wouldn't fight at her wedding. Would you be willing to commit to not expressing these feelings in the midst of gatherings for the sake of your children's peace and well-being? What would help make this possible for you?)

 • I feel:

 • The reasons for these feelings are:

B. Think about why I am still unable to speak to the other parent. (Unless I fear bodily harm, I will consider talking with a counselor, religious leader, trusted wise person, or a trained mediator about my continuing anger, hurt, grief, or disappointment. Should it make sense to both of us, I will seek to include the other parent in conversations with a third party about how we might be civil during events where we both desire to be present.):

C. Be careful how I speak to my child about my former mate's new relationship. I have these thoughts and feelings about that person:

D. Accept that my children are loving people and given that, I know they might come to care deeply about that new person. Do I believe that my children have enough love for all of us?

E. Reassure my children that I love them and that I believe they are capable of long-term relationships and being good parents, if that is their dream. I will think carefully about the kinds of things I say about being in relationships. Do I make positive or negative remarks?

For further reading I suggest:
- Hetherington, E. Mavis, and John Kelly. *For Better or For Worse: Divorce Reconsidered.* New York: W. W. Norton & Company, 2002.
- Wallerstein, Judith S., Julia M. Lewis, and Sandra Blakeslee. *The Unexpected Legacy of Divorce: A 25 Year Landmark Study.* New York: Hyperion, 2000.

6. THE HOUR I SPEND WITH GOD

WONDERING is what children of the switching hour do as they talk and ask questions about their lives with the One who is Holy.

Because I am willing to see life from my child's point of view, I will:

A. Listen patiently to his or her questions about the Holy One and ponder my own thoughts and feelings about the Holy One, religion, and the community of faith. Some thoughts and feelings that come to mind are:

B. Consider whether my religious community has helped or harmed me during this time of separation or divorce. What has hurt me? What has helped me? How is this affecting my children? Am I willing to share this book with my religious leader?

C. Acknowledge feelings of shame, guilt, anger, confusion, or hurt that I may have and seek out a religious leader or trusted wise person in order to discuss these feelings with him or her:

D. Discuss the religious upbringing of my child with the other parent. (Children often benefit from having other interested adults in their lives such as those found in trustworthy religious communities. Yes, unfortunately, it is important to see if those in charge have had criminal background checks and if the community implements safe practices with children. Religious communities should not be offended if you ask about these issues. After having asked those questions, don't worry about *making a mistake* when selecting a religion. The children will change religious connections when they are older, if they are not at home in this religion. There are long-term benefits of a positive faith foundation in childhood, regardless of sect or denomination. The book, *Honoring Our Neighbor's Faith*, gives an overview of various religions.)
   • What would keep me from doing this?

E. Allow my children to ask religious questions, even if I do not wish to be a religious person. I will support my children's religious life.
  • What might this require of me? Am I ready to take my child to services that I do not attend? I will do what is required of me in order to keep this commitment, such as:

For further reading I suggest:
  • Farlee, Robert Buckley, editor. *Honoring Our Neighbor's Faith.* Augsburg Fortress, 1999.
  • Marquardt, Elizabeth. *Between Two Worlds: The Inner Lives of Children of Divorce.* New York: Crown Publishers, 2005.

WE CARE

Finally, what you can do to help is approach parenting with attitudes and behaviors that say *WE CARE.* In two words, WE CARE highlights the core of the divided lives of children and communicates to the children that their switching hour life matters. Caring parents are willing to hear difficult and painful stories from their children. They are committed to making the lives of their children less upsetting or stressful.

Waiting describes much of what the children of the switching hour do. They wait to be picked up. They wait to return to the other parent. Some-times they wait for parents to just get along. Parents who say **WE CARE** are on time and coordinate with the other parent.

Effort is required of children who are continually on the move. Those of you who travel regularly for work or pleasure know the effort it takes to keep track of all your belongings. When children are making connections with people who may be sad or angry, it requires even more energy. Children are undergoing physical changes; that takes extra energy by itself. Parents who say **WE CARE** try to reduce the stress for our children. They provide time for adequate rest and relaxation.

Changes fill the life of the child of the switching hour. Life is not how they expected it would be. Now they have two places to call home. Mom and Dad have new lives, perhaps new loves. How do the children express their pain and anger without upsetting the parents? What if Mom doesn't let me see her anymore? Parents who say **WE CARE** are sensitive to the pain of changes in our children's lives.

Absence is the core experience of the kids of the switching hour—when they are with one parent, they will always be away from the other parent—except for rare occasions if the parents are cooperative. They say good-bye again and again. Parents who say **WE CARE** are present for our children and understanding about their longing for the absent parent.

Relationships with both parents are crucial for a child's well-being. A good relationship with both of one's parents means everything to a child. While this is not always possible, as in the case of dangerous parents or those who desert their families, it is the desire of a child's heart to have a father *and* a mother who love them.

When a divorce occurs, other relationships change in the child's life as well. The network of classmates, teammates, neighborhood friends, and extended families may change as well. Being a caring parent means that effort is expended in helping your children remain connected with those they care about. You are training them to value relationships and by doing so, they will be strengthened in relating to you as well. Parents who say **WE CARE** model positive relationships.

Ease – Easing the stress in his or her switching hour life shows your child you care. Parents who *say* **WE CARE** continually look for new ways to *show* our children that **WE CARE**.

Living in ways that show **WE CARE** as divorced parents will make your children feel loved and understood. A friend of mine demonstrated this beautifully. We were gathered for a Fourth of July picnic. There were all kinds of games and food. Harry and his son, Jason, were enjoying the rodeo, golf, and swimming. The hour arrived when Jason had to leave and go to his mother's home so that he could attend a Renaissance Fair with her and his maternal grandmother. I heard him tell Harry, "I really would like to swim some more." The party was still in full swing and I could see the desire to remain and the desire to go to be with his mom bumping up against each other. "Okay," said Harry, "call me when you're done at the fair, and I'll come back and get you so you can swim some more." Jason called later and Harry gladly made the forty-mile round trip once again. Jason was full of smiles when he was back in the pool. I was so grateful to witness this father giving his son the gift of relationships; it means everything because he has the **WE CARE** spirit.

Be Switching Hour parents who say, "WE CARE."

I hope that by reading the truth of the stories in this book, you have been able to take the child's point of view, hear your children in new ways, and use your deepened understanding to ease the stress of children who live the switching hour life by saying and demonstrating that WE CARE each and every day.

The Switching Hour

Time is
Too Slow for those who Wait,
Too Swift for those who Fear,
Too Long for those who Grieve,
Too Short for those who Rejoice,
But for those who Love,
Time is Not.
—Henry Van Dyke, "For Katrina's Sun-Dial"